Rapture and the Left Behind

FULL ARMOR
BOOKS

Rapture and the Left behind

Published by Full Armor Books

Wrote by Elijah K

Edited by Jay Kim

Designed by Julia Lee

Email address_ etmmin@gmail.com

ISBN 979-11-961182-4-2

Rapture and the Left Behind

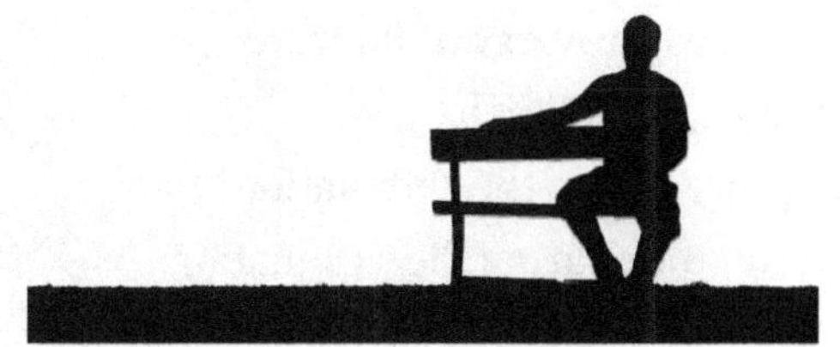

ELIJAH H.K

CONTENTS

One day in February 2012, I was able to hear the voice of the Lord after seven years of his last voice. I am not a frequent listener of the voice of God, so I remember the day correctly. On that day, the Holy Spirit gave the words to my heart with a very soft voice. It says, "Wake up. You shall awaken my people." From that night on, I have been studying materials related to the end times for the last few years. I went to study in the United States, spent much money, earned a degree, worked in the media field, and taught students in college. The Lord has told me to put down all thoughts of personal success and prepare his ministry. I was very embarrassed. I was afraid of living a life in full of suffering and not getting married as an old bachelor.

After lots of thought, I called my mother and told her I could not expect a materially wealthy life or a marriage anymore. I said I should wake up the Lord's brides until Jesus comes. My mother, first wordless, has become a warrior of prayer and has been helping me as intercessory prayer. Through this article, I would like to express my gratitude to my mother and the intercessor team members. Now I am writing this book after putting down all my desire and living a life with happiness and thanksgiving with a beautiful wife and my lovely son.

I have held several seminars while preparing a ministry with a book called "The War of Darkness." After the workshops, the most frequent questions I had to answer were about the 'rapture and the left behind.' Since I do not know the day and the hour, the most crucial question is whether they will be taken to the rapture or left behind. So far, I have done much research on this subject as I was writing a book about the end times and holding a seminar. In this book, I have summarized the things the Holy Spirit has inspired me as I was praying and studying for several years.

Who are the first ones, the left-behinds in the Old Testament? Who are the left-behinds in the Gospels, Epistles, and Revelation? I studied those who were taken to the rapture and those who were left behind. The Bible repeatedly records those who are taken away to avoid tribulation, those who are left alive and those who are abandoned and destroyed. God wants us to read the Bible and realize this. These topics begin with Genesis. It is about the tribulations and the rapture in stories of Enoch and Noah, Abraham and Lots. Such as Jacob and Joseph, Moses, Joshua, Naomi and Ruth, Elijah and Elisha, three friends of Daniel, Mordecai, and Esther, Jesus and his disciples, the Church of Jerusalem and the Gentile church and the book of Revelation.

In Luke chapter 17, the Pharisees ask Jesus about the kingdom of God. They are very curious about when the kingdom of God will come. The Pharisees, who were proficient in the Old Testament, believed that when the kingdom of God comes, they could gain a high status in the mighty nation of Israel as Isaiah and Ezekiel prophesied. Jesus said that the kingdom of God would happen as soon as lightning flashes. On that day, destruction will come to earth like Sodom and Gomorrah, and those who will be saved will be taken away from there. Jesus tells the story of a man who lived at home, a man who worked with mills, and a man who plowed fields. One of them will be taken away, and the others will be left behind.

Jesus told them that it would be like Sodom and Gomorrah, and the Pharisees again wondered where this would happen. When the disciples asked, "Where,

Lord?" in Luke verse 17:37, Jesus speaks unexpectedly. "Wherever there is a dead body, an eagle is gathered together." The Pharisees were interested in what would be happened in Israel, but in fact, Jesus was responding that this event would occur anywhere in the world. There is a reason why the Gospel of Luke recorded this story in detail. Luke was a gentile with a literary character, as well as medical knowledge, navigation, and familiar with the Greek. The apostle Paul expressed Luke as a beloved physician (Colossians 4:14).

Luke was Paul's disciple, companion, and family doctor. Unlike other Gospels, Luke tells a story about the salvation of the stranger from the viewpoint of the Gentiles. Unlike the Gospel of Matthew, Luke describes the genealogy from Jesus, the Savior of all, to Adam, the ancestor of humankind. Luke records in detail that Jesus plans to save the Gentiles as well as the Jews.

Jesus is saying that disasters will appear not only in Judea but all over the world such as those that occurred in Sodom and Gomorrah at the time of trouble. Those who are taken away are the brides who will participate in the marriage feast of the Lamb, and those who are abandoned are the less prepared brides. (Matthew 25: 1-12) Those who were left behind are many who would die, and eagles would eat their bodies. Eagles and birds also serve to feed the masses of those who rebel against God in Revelation. In Deuteronomy 28:26, it is written that those who disobey God will be cursed and become the food of birds and beasts.

Those who are left behind can be divided into three classes. The first is the Lord's brides who are not ready. They are the fools in Matthew chapter 25 those who are lazy and not awaken. They do not use the talents that the Lord has given them. The second is those who are prepared to be called for left behind as shown in Joel 2:32. They are like two witnesses left with the power of God to make people who are left behind to pass the Tribulation safely. The third category is those who do not believe but have survived on the earth without receiving the mark of the beast. During the tribulation, the Beast influence on one-third of the Earth. Apart from this, the people living in the remote regions and those who resist the Beast, especially the Jews, belong to this third class. God has a beautiful plan of salvation for those who are left behind in this third category.

This book summarizes some of the words about it. Recently, American novelists and film and drama producers are creating content related to the Left Behind. It tells us that people's interest in the rapture is growing. There are many specific prophecies about those who are left behind in the Bible. Those who have wisdom will have to live a holy life using the words of the Bible as a lesson so that they will not be left behind on earth in the day of the wrath of God. The purpose of writing this book is to tell that we must be holy in order not to be left behind. But not all those who are left will die but will be treated like gold as refined through fire. (Zechariah13: 9)

I have taught my disciples in college for many years. Among the disciples, there is always a class of disobedient, lazy and rebellious to the professor. During the semester, I persevere for a long time without penalizing these students. However, as a professor, I feel rewarded when I judge these students were giving F after the final exam. Judgment and reward are systems that can be done in a little human world. God has endured mortal sin and disobedience for a long time. However, we should remember that the Judgment day will come during that period of rage. The Bible deals with God's love, salvation, and judgment. However, Christians emphasize only the love of God and do not know about the decision. The Bible goes into detail about the judgment of God. I hope you will meditate on the Bible day and night and look up to God's salvation and wisdom and be prepared as the Lord's beautiful bride.

And except those days should be shortened,

there should no flesh be saved:

but for the elect's sake,

those days should all be shortened.

Matthew 24:22

Part I

"Left Behind"

And the dragon was wroth with the woman

and went to make war with the remnant of her seed, which

keeps the commandments of God,

and have the testimony of Jesus Christ

Revelation 12:17

Who is the left behind?

God makes a covenant with Noah. (Genesis 8:21) Noah's descendants will become great and fill the earth again. After the next seven years of tribulation, when Jesus returns, the earth's population will be replenished by the descendants of those who were left, as in the days of Noah. Those who survive and endure to the end of the remnant will multiply by the grace of God and become the inhabitants of the millennial kingdom. The Bible predicts that during the seven-year tribulation, more than half of the earth's population will die. Huge blood and loud weeping sound will cover the ground. In the wilderness where Moses led the Jews, hundreds of people die each day. Those who are left behind also will suffer when they see people around them die every day. Those who are left will also be held captive by the Beast army and will have to run away to survive. Those who are left will suffer from hunger every day and will suffer from cold and heat. However, those who are left will endure 1,260 days from where God has prepared them. That period is a refine of fire that those who are left behind will have to pass through.

After they have passed through the fire refinement, they will come out like pure gold and be reborn as the holy God's people. Those who are left will be protected by the wings of God's great eagle. We will see the supernatural power of the Lord every day by being supplied with the necessary foods. Those who are left will not have to wash their clothes and buy new shoes. The only desire of those who are left is to meditate, pray, and praise God's Word. Life is so simple that you will only be devoting yourself every day, except the movements and actions necessary to survive. Those left ones are blessed to see, hear, and feel the many prophecies recorded in the book of Revelation in their own eyes.

Those who are left will experience every prophecy recorded in the book of Revelation, so they will be the people who will understand the revelations more than anyone else and keep the words. Those who want to see all the great earthquakes and the second coming of Jesus on earth can be the left behind to experience all this vividly. However, mental and physical pain will follow. When Jesus offered himself as a sacrifice of the lamb of the Passover, he went through extreme pain and abandonment. Those who remain will be the protagonists of the book of Revelation, but they will have to join in the suffering of Jesus with neglect. Those who have been raptured have already suffered these kinds of pains in their lives. They have participated in the suffering of Jesus and are holy people who have already received the refine of fire. Those who have joined the rapture are those who do not need to be left behind. Jesus' disciples must choose one of two things. They must choose whether to live a life joining Christ's suffering in the present life or to be left after the rapture to pass through the refining of fire.

The Bible repeatedly speaks about those who remain, from Genesis to Revelation. In Genesis, Noah and his family are the most representative of those who are left behind. Adam and Eve lived 930 years after they were born and continued to give birth to their children. Seth also lived 912 years and continues to have children. Enos, the son of Seth, lived 905 years and bore children. There is speculation that more than 10 billion people would have lived in the days of Enoch, the righteous person of Genesis. Scientists speculate that the depth of the ocean was 200 to 300 meters lower than it is now, so the population had a much better environment for living. At that time, the earth was a good environment for growing trees and plants; therefore huge forests and trees bearing fruits would have been growing well.

At the time of Enoch, the fall of angels caused sin to spread into human beings like cancer cells. Fallen angels escape from their dwellings and take human ladies and give birth to the Nephilim, the Giants. The Nephilim has a powerful muscle. According to 'the book of Enoch' and 'the book of the Jasher' which enjoyed by the rabbis of Judaism, the mixed race of angels and humans, Nephilim, is sturdy, hunted, and has the eating habit of human beings. The Nephilim caught the ladies and made them sexual slaves of their own, even making animals for sexual objects. The rebellion of the Nephilim and angels caused the human world to fall into an evil and fallen path. God lamented that he had made man and he was anxious in his heart. In the end, God has decided to judge humans by water. The greatest sin that Nephilim has committed is to make a hybrid of humans and animals to create a monster-shaped child.

This sin was widespread by evil angels who knew not the science and technology of the day but the secrets of magic, spiritual power, and the creation. God urged the world to notice their sins through Enoch. The people of those days ignored the teachings of Enoch and even taunted the prophets. God teaches Enoch the secret that the death of his son Methuselah is the beginning of judgment. Since Enoch's direct descendants received these teachings, they sought to live godly and holy. Methuselah also lives in 969 years with the grace of God as a result of being devoted to his Father's will. Lamech, son of Methuselah, teaches the will of his father to his son Noah. Noah went to the home of his grandfather, Methuselah, from his childhood, and was educated.

The Book of Jasher, quoted in Joshua chapter 10 and Samuel chapter 1, says when Adam died, many of his descendants participated in the burial, crying and buried his body on the ground, which was the beginning of a funeral culture. Their father and ancestors especially give the descendants of Adam the faith. Abraham, too, was told by his father, Terah, that he had received his belief in the house of his grandfather, Noah when he was a child. The ancestors of faith who had already set an example of confidence before the law of Moses all owe to Enoch's teachings. Enoch is the first person to be raptured, walking with God, fighting against evil Nephilim, and crying out the will of God through all his life for righteous. It would have been his son, Methuselah, who was shocked after Enoch's rapture. He would have been more insightful in his father's words that humans would be judged by water after his death.

Methuselah would have been concerned that his son Lamech would be left after his death. However, Lamech dies five years earlier than Methuselah, as 192 years younger than his father. By the grace of God, Lamech would pass without trouble. However, God commands Noah to make an ark 120 years before the death of Methuselah. Noah was already able to follow the command of God because his grandfather had taught him, Methuselah and his father Lamech, to make the ark. Noah begins to train his three sons because he knew the judgment of the water would come after 120 years when his grandfather, Methuselah dies. Noah teaches his son well to meet a good spouse with faith. Now, 120 years can be felt very long for us, but I guess the time was not long enough for Noah that he had to prepare many things in that period.

People could easily think that God made all the materials Noah needed lumbers and a boat in a flash. However, Noah prepared for 120 years according to God's command. God is the one who commands man and watches whether he obeys the Word. Therefore, prayer's response sometimes appears to be slow. Noah sincerely prepared all the gopher wood, the necessary utensils, and the food. The bitumen used as a waterproof material would have had to come to the land of Sinar (Babylon area) and hardly float. The sons of Noah, companions of the faith, would have worked hard to obey the will of their father. The time has finally arrived. Seven days before the death of his grandfather, Methuselah, God gives it to Noah in advance. (Genesis 7: 4) From now on, the countdown begins every day.

Jesus said that until the day the Noah entered the ark before the Flood, people did not realize the destruction. (Matthew 24:39) Jesus' second coming to the future will also come at a time when people will not recognize the damage at all. In the 1 Thessalonians 5:3, Paul says that destruction is happening at a moment when people think that "the world is peaceful and safe." The point of the rapture is that humans will not notice at all.

Noah's name means 'to rest.' At the time of judgment, Noah can rest with the grace of God. No one knows when Jesus will return. However, the awaken man could tell when the thief came. (Matthew 24:43, 1 Thessalonians 5: 4) Here the thief is the appearance of the Antichrist. Those who are awake will never lose Jesus from thieves. They will be prepared like Noah and led to the resting place of Goshen.

Those who are left behind are those who are not raptured, remain on the earth like Noah and endure judgment. Some of those who are saved from those who are left are receiving God's grace during the tribulation, so they should never be disappointed. They must try to keep themselves and their families like Noah. At the time of judgment, we will lose all social relations, material, status, and home. With that pain, you may need to sleep in wine like Noah. Those who are left may think that God temporarily abandoned them because they could not be raptured. However, being left is not a curse. Those who are left will experience God's salvation plan, grace, and amazing supernatural power. Those who are left behind have responsibility for the souls of the rest. Noah is not the servant of God who was forsaken.

The typical type of the Rapture before the Tribulation in the Bible is Enoch's Rapture. The other is the rapture of Elijah's during the tribulation. Elijah was a prophet who had suffered from distress. Elijah had to go through the ordeal of the drought for three and a half years hid in the cave of mountain Horeb, avoiding the severe persecution of Jezebel. Elijah strengthened by the fact that God has hidden the seven thousand men and he begins ministry again. He went to Damascus in the north and anointed Hazael, and went down again, anointed with oil to Jehu in the northern kingdom of Israel, and went back to Elisha, who lived in Abel-meholah and made disciples of him. Ahab's successor, King Ahaziah, sent the soldiers to kill Elijah, but with the supernatural power of God, they are all burned.

When Elisha grows up to some extent, Elijah makes his last trip to his disciples. Elijah went to Gilgal, which symbolized the Word of God and the holy circumcision, to give Elisha a silent lesson. He also went to a fallen city Bethel where built an idol. In Jericho, symbolizing marching to the Canaan, he took a whirlwind and raptured in front of Elisha. Elijah may want Elisha to restore the house of God and to save Israel, saying, "O people! I would like to leave a message, 'Go back to God again.'

Elisha saw his teacher raptured to heaven, while there was envy on the one hand and on the other side that had to worry about things to go on. The only thing Elisha could ask for was his ability to double portion for winning through the tribulation of Israel. During his long ministry, Elisha had to go through a rough history of devastating war, murder, famine, and eating human flesh. He saw the iniquity of the northern kingdom of Israel and the southern kingdom of Judah, and the killing of many kings and royalty. To keep the disciples of left behind, Elisha also ran a prophetic school and were responsible for their families. He had to stop the army of the mighty Syrian and turn the iniquity of the northern kingdom of Israel into a ministry that would not be destroyed by the cruel Assyria that will arise in the future.

Elisha's life was much more dramatic than Elijah and needed much help from God. The left Elisha receives double the power of Elijah from God. Elisha required more ability than Elijah to fulfill the duty of those who were left behind. He worked to wake the king of Israel until just before his death, but it was not enough. The Jews disobeyed the words of the prophets who were amid the idolatrous sin and prophesying of God. Elisha is antitype for the abilities of those who will be left in the future and the many trials that must pass. Spending many chapters in the Bible and showing the record of Elisha is because there is a special message to those who are left behind.

God's Time Table

Revelation tells us about the ministry of the two witnesses. The two witnesses call for Israel's recovery and repentance for three and a half years. The forces of Satan try to kill two witnesses, but the two witnesses who have been given authority continue to minister until the hundred and forty-four thousand of sealed ones come out. The power of the two witnesses cause the failure of rain for three and a half years in Israel and disasters happen. Because of the prophecy and ministry of the two witnesses, the stubborn people who are thirsty hate both witnesses and their followers. At the end of the three and a half years of power of the two witnesses, the Beast that will rule over post three and a half years will appear, killing both witnesses and their followers. Martyrdom of the two witnesses and a hundred and forty-four thousand who are forehead sealed happens. However, two witnesses and a hundred and forty-four thousand are resurrected three days after their death and are raptured before many people see them. When two witnesses and their followers are raptured, there will be a great earthquake in the city of Israel, and seven thousand people will die.

The Jews who saw the events of the two witnesses and their followers being resurrected and raptured were shocked to believe in Jesus. They are the Jews who are left behind. The Jews who have come to believe in Jesus are those who will be subjected to get through the next three and a half years of great tribulation. The Bible says that they will spend 1,260 days in the place that God has prepared. The two witnesses and the rapture of a hundred and forty-four thousand people would be the first fruits that make many Jews believe in Jesus. The immediate object of Revelation is sending the message of salvation to the Jews, and the expanding purpose is sending the message to us, the Gentiles. Those who are 'left behinds' are messages to Jews and Gentiles. At first, a hundred and forty-four thousand Jews get sealed, and the first rapture and salvation of the Gentiles come (Rev. 7: 9). After that, the Rapture of two witnesses (including a hundred and forty-four thousand sealed) (Revelation 11:12) will happen. Soon after, more gentiles will be raptured. (Revelation 15:16) The Bible says that there is a rapture before the tribulation for the first fruits and a rapture during the ordeal for many fruits. Therefore, there are two raptures in the Bible.

In Revelation chapter 7, the Jews are represented by a limited number of a hundred and forty-four thousand, but the Gentiles are many. However, by the first fruits of a hundred and forty-four thousand, many Jews will not bow down to the Beast and endure to the end, and those who have overcome will see Jesus. The Bible records God's fantastic plan to save the Jews. The Gentiles have a high spiritual debt to the Jews. God first filled the fullness of the Gentiles for the salvation of the Jews. The Gentiles are saved according to the Bible written by the Jews and their incredible knowledge of God. Therefore, the Gentiles should do their best to help Israel for the salvation of the Jews.

Elisha helps the king and does his best to prevent Israel from falling. He serves those who are left with the power, faith, and warm heart of his own. Those who remain among the Gentiles like Elisha must fight against the World Beast Government, the union of the Antichrist. The left and the nations of the east must resist to the end against the World Beast Government and must ally with Israel. Those who are left among the Gentiles must pray for the rest of the Israelites and reach out for help. When the time comes, God's hand will destroy the headquarters of the World Beast Government.

The World Beast Government will win the war at first

against the union of the remaining, but it will become weaker and weaker, and later it will be gathered in the plains of Megiddo (Armageddon) on the north side of Jerusalem. The time will come when the governments of the remaining gathering all their military forces to attack the armies of the World Beast Government gathered in Megiddo. Then the end of the Great War is coming. Jesus who waits so long is coming down from heaven with his army. People around the world will see Jesus riding a white horse and wearing red blood-sprayed clothes. The believers who have seen the image of Jesus will pour out the tears of joy, but the sinners will weep.

The sword-like word that comes out of Jesus' mouth causes the enemy's army to stop and split their heart. An army descending from heaven removes the remnants of the Beast Army for the millennial kingdom to make everything into the first year of God's Jubilee year. It called the beginning of the Millennium kingdom. All the powers and systems created by man are restored to perfection. The temple of Ezekiel will be built again in Jerusalem. God's feast will be restored, and everything will return to the original. The water from the Ezekiel temple flows into the sea and heals the water that has turned into blood during the tribulation. All nations will visit the temple of Ezekiel in Jerusalem to keep the feast of tabernacles. Those who remain in the millennium kingdom are to learn and to train the word of God. Just like the Jews who came back from Babylonian captivity and read the Word and repented.

In Malachi, God commands to read and practice Leviticus again for those who are left behind from Babylonian captivity. The background of Malachi is the last word of God to the Jews who settled after the Babylonian captivity. Since then, God has been silent for about 400 years. In the meantime, the Jews will experience many things. Before they meet Jesus, they are confused by aggressions and wars with many nations. In the time of the millennial kingdom, God demands that we return to the word of Leviticus again, like the background in Malachi. The temple of Ezekiel is made, holy law rules the world and democracy and capitalism will be disappeared. The Leviticus period of the millennial kingdom is the same as before except for the law of sacrifices and the circumcision of the flesh. It is because the covenant of God is the same as the past, the present, and the future.

At the end of the millennial kingdom, the Great War will occur again, and many were prophesied to be deceived and to rebel against God. At the end of the judgment, all of them will stand before the great white throne as sinners. At the end of the millennial kingdom, both Jesus and his royal priests would complete their mission and go up to paradise. Jesus' disciples rule the millennial kingdom with love and justice, but as the time passes and Satan is released from the abyss, and many will fall. Biblically Gog and Magog are farthest away from Jerusalem, the center of the earth. It means that the weakest place to the Bible. There is rebellion in the Gog and Magog area, and the last war in the world happens again. The ones who fall are the weak ones to the Bible. We must arm ourselves properly by studying the Word, Bible during the millennium.

Maranatha

Those who were left after the New Testament period were Jesus' disciples and early Church believers. The ordinary disciples later become apostles. At the time of Roman persecution and tribulation, all of Jesus' disciples would receive the same power and prophetic ministry as Elisha. Through the efforts of the apostles, the gospel is preached in Jerusalem, Asia Minor, Greece, and Rome, and later spread into India and Asia. The apostles gave all of themselves with faith in Jesus who would come again. The early church members also lived holy in community life. They did not deny Jesus even in the persecution of Rome, and they even gave their lives to God. Those who have not been martyred have hidden in the underground graves or the mountains and have kept the Word and faith of God. Those who were left in the early persecution made seven beautiful churches in the book of Revelation.

The Church serves as a refuge where the remaining are nurtured and protected. The Church serves as the mother of the believers. It becomes the body of Jesus under the protection of angels. The church is a beautiful gold candlestick which is the body with all the seven spirits of the Holy Spirit. If the church disobeys, the candlestick will be moved. The church where the candlestick is moved becomes the church where the Holy Spirit has left. The church becomes a fortress where the believers can only rely on and survive when the world persecutes. The church is the sheepfold of the lamb who feeds with the word of God. The door for the sheep is Jesus. The good shepherd keeps his sheep for his life. However, the hireling shepherd's greed for money, and when the threat of the world comes, they abandon the sheep and run away. The wise sheep should move to a church with a good shepherd. In Revelation 18: 4, God's people do not take part in the sin, but instead, come out of it.

Roman Catholicism is not a church. The church is the place where there is a good shepherd and where the seven spirits of the Holy Spirit come together. The Early Church did not recognize Roman Catholicism as a church from the beginning because of idolatry and goddess worship. The early church has remained an underground church for many years, avoiding the persecution of Roman Catholicism. When Jesus came back, the Holy Spirit was poured out. The sudden revival of the church from the nineteenth century is the total grace of God that pours out because the time of Jesus' coming is near. It is a wrong idea that the church has escaped from the Roman Catholic Church. Rather, the church is more like the early church than the Roman Catholic. The church should strive to be more like the early church of the Jews left behind after Jesus' ascension.

Orthodox Jews believe in the God of the Old Testament and do not recognize Jesus as the Messiah. On the other hand, Messianic Jews think that the Messiah of the Old Testament and the New Testament is Jesus. However, they refuse to become Western-style Christians. Messianic Jews want to reject the evil customs and theology of the Western church and return to the early church. Modern churches must listen to the opinions of Messianic Jews. Christians are Jesus like people from the perspective of the Western church. However, the Jews are looking at Jesus, the Messiah, from the standpoint of the Jews. A church all around the world should also discern what the wrong church customs and theologies of the West are, and see what is wrong with the biblical standard, and discard what is not right. Because it is not to pleases a person, but to please God. The unbiblical content of alternative theology, glorious theology, liberal theology, prosperity theology, love theology, law abolition, and A-Millennialism must be boldly discarded. The fullness of the Gentiles surpasses the customs, thoughts, and beliefs of the Jews, and gentiles must live a good life of faith for to provoke Jews to jealousy. (Roman 11:11)

This era in which Messianic Jews are increasing is close to the end time. Because after the full number of the Gentiles to be saved is filled, then the amount of the Jews is filled up to a hundred and forty-four thousand. The countdown towards the end time has begun. In recent years, the books and teachings of Pastor Messianic Jews have challenged many Gentiles. From the Jewish point of view, especially from Genesis to Revelation, it helps us to read and understand the Bible as a whole. God told us to eat the whole body of the lamb in the Passover. It means to eat the entire thing instead of eating only the part where you like the word of God, which is the spiritual food given by God. When we look at the Bible as a whole, the minds of the Jews are read and understood. The churches of all around should help and serve the Jewish church in the last days. God's concern is in the Jews and those left behind in oppressed countries. God tells us to return to the Word so the Church will not be reproved.

The church of all around, which is the fence of the remaining people, is facing a great crisis now. The next generations are not going to church anymore. The churches built with much debt will suffer from tremendous financial difficulties soon. Young people are losing faith and respect for the church. Furthermore, the church is treated as hostile as the old generation. The media is becoming increasingly evil, causing young people' deviation and media addiction. The Bible shows that if gays gather together like an army, the land will have perished. However, every year in June, gays are gathering like an army parade at many major world cities. The church does not stop them, nor does it inform the believers. When the church disappears, where do the remaining people get nurtured? The church is the last bastion to which the remaining can trust.

There is a way for the church to live again. It is so simple for the shepherds to go back to the Bible. We must read and preach the Word from Genesis to Revelation as a whole. Like David, the church building must be prepared slowly with prayer after saving in advance. Media Fasting helps young people and the next generation to survive spiritually. Larger churches need to keep their finances and pay off their debts in advance. College student missions must be resurrected. There must be a Bible movement in university again. The revival of worship should go with the recovery of the Word. It is a mistake listening to contemporary Christian music (CCM) every day but not to study the Bible. Faith is to go with the act. The helmet of salvation must not be taken away until the end of the mission. The church needs to return to the Word again in preparation for the end time.

The end time church will be a time of sheep and goat separation, but at the same time, a great opportunity will be given. However, the church that is only in the toast of prosperity and material will inevitably fall. After the period of wealth, the trials of the world will surely come. War and famine will come to the world in unbearable hardship, but the church will be a comfort and a shield for those who are left behind. The church should encourage those who are left after the rapture to have faith again without despair. It should also be a useful guide for them to pass the tribulation correctly. The church should save like Joseph in the prosperous times, preparing for the time of trial. It must also be the servant of the praiseworthy God who gives food to the poor in times of trouble.

The church should pray for the government. We also must always pray for the peace of Israel. We must pray for the anti-Beast army to win the war. The church must provide food, drink water, and clothing to keep your neighbors from starving. Furthermore, the church should pray for their country to play the role of the land of Goshen.

Moreover, it should be holier than the other religions of believing in any gods, and the church members must be dignified. The church must be a spiritual shield to prevent enemy attacks by prayer. When the vial catastrophe is poured out, the land of Goshen gains strength. Then the church increases power. The church should pray to reclaim Jerusalem from its enemies for the left and the army of God. We must also desire the kingdom of Jesus Christ and the Messiah to come back to proclaim the word of God every day.

**"Blessed is he who comes
In the name of the Lord."**

"He which testifies these things say,

Surely, I come quickly.

Amen. Even so, come, Lord Jesus "

Revelation 22:20

Part II

"Rapture"

Then we which are alive and remain shall be

caught up together with them in the clouds,

to meet the Lord in the air: and so shall

We ever be with the Lord

1 Thessalonians 4:17

The theological controversy of Rapture

It is called 'rapture during the tribulation' that being raptured after the seventh trumpet is sounded. Also, I call it 'Elijah rapture.' The most controversial theologians are the rapture events in Revelation chapter 7 and chapter 14. The rapture is either before the tribulation (Chapter 7) or during the tribulation (Chapter 14). Some class is claiming that only chapter 7 is the rapture case and another class is claiming that only chapter 14 is the rapture case. I claim that there are two raptures in chapters seven and fourteen. Because the book of Revelation is recorded in chronological order, a detailed explanation of this can be found in my book "God's Timetable; The TimeLine." After the first rapture of the first fruits, there is a full-scale second rapture, called great harvest. The order is as follows. 1. The seal of the Jews is determined. 2. Next, the Gentiles are prepared for the rapture. 3. Two witnesses and a hundred and forty-four thousand will be raptured after ministering for three and a half years, and then resurrected after being dead. 4. At the same time, many gentiles are massively raptured by angels. 5. After that, those of the Jews and the Gentiles should endure fighting or escaping the Beast for three and a half years.

The "Rapture" Timeline of Revelation follows in this order. 1. Seal disaster 2. Trumpet disaster. 3. Vial disaster. The target of the most severe vial disaster is the Antichrist government and his army, not the ones left behind. When the vial is poured out, there will be a great disaster for the cities, the military facilities, and the wicked, where the reign of the beast. Like the Pharaoh in Exodus and the ten catastrophes, his country has received. Believers avoid death by merely applying the blood of the lamb to the door. Those who are left believe in Jesus Christ and use the blood on the doorposts of the heart. Those who have been left will receive the supernatural power and protection of the Lord as Elisha has experienced for the three and a half years. It is recorded in the Bible.

Rapture of Enoch and Elijah

There is no direct word in the Bible about the rapture, but there are many terms with similar meanings. The Bible tells us about the distinction between those who believe in God and those who do not believe. Believers are sheep, and those who do not believe are goats. The sheep are distinguished and resurrected into a new heaven and a new earth. However, the goat is resurrected for judgment and falls forever in the Lake of fire. The sheep, the children of God, who are dead or alive, will be saved forever. The rapture is a term used synonymously for the phenomena in which the children of God are alienated and saved. In the Gospels, Jesus showed himself being raptured before his disciples.

Enoch and Elijah are the people who are raptured in the Bible. In the rapture of Enoch and Elijah, the believers receive many messages. Enoch is a representative figure of the rapture before the Tribulation, and Elijah is the representative who gets the rapture during the Tribulation. In the Old Testament, Elisha is a type of resurrection. As soon as the body of the Moabite thief who was killed in the invasion of Israel is thrown into the grave, it reaches the bone of Elisha. (2 Kings 13:21) Elisha's bones became the mediator of resurrection. The Bible records the resurrection. Jesus shows us how he died after suffering a tribulation and then resurrected and lived again and raptured. Prophets like Enoch, Elijah, and Elisha have symbolized all types of Jesus.

All the characters and events in the Old Testament are the testimony to Jesus. Like Enoch, believers may be raptured before the tribulation, or like Elijah, raptured during the ordeal. Like Elisha, you may go through all the trial, then die, and resurrect for the rapture. The believers are not aware of the time of their rapture but must recognize that there is rapture through the Bible. Let me look at some words related to the rapture in the

Bible. In Exodus 6: 6-8, God promises the Israelites five things.

1. I will bring you out (yatsa) from under the burdens of the Egyptians.
2. I will rid (natsal) you out of their bondage,
3. I will redeem (ga'al) you with a stretched-out arm, and with great judgments.
4. I will take (laqach) you to me for my people.
5. I will lead (bo) you to land I swore to give it to Abraham, Isaac, and Jacob and will give it to you as a heritage.

In Hebrew, "yacha" means removed from the status of a servant. People who believe in Jesus are no longer slaves but sons. The word "natsal" means being saved or rescued. In Hebrew, "Jesus" means the Savior. There is only Jesus who saves us. 'ga'al' means paying off and redeem. Jesus paid for our sins and redeemed life for us.

In Hebrew, 'laqach' means to take it with you. It is recorded in Genesis 5:24 that God 'laqach' Enoch. In 2 Kings 2: 3 and 2 Kings 2: 10-11, it is stated that God 'laqach' Elijah. 'Laqach' is used as the direct Hebrew language of the rapture. When translated from the New Testament into Greek, laqach is expressed 'harfazo' in 1 Thessalonians 4:17. Harpazo means to take it and take it away. The apostle Paul used harpazo as a means of rapture in the air. The apostle John also used the harpazo in Revelation 12: 5 for the son of the woman to go up before God and his throne.

The Hebrew word 'bo' means 'movement in space' from one place to another. 'Bo' tells us that God will deliver the Israelites out of the land of Egypt into Canaan, the Promised Land. God delivers the believer from an evil world like Egypt or Babylon to a new heaven and a new earth, the Promised Land. Isaiah 26:20 says, "Let my people go into the chamber, shut your door, and hide for a moment before the wrath of God passes." The secret room is expressed as a place of hiding before the wrath of God passes. One of the great pastors of the Methodist Church said that "The Bible is about the escape." The Bible repeatedly tells God's people not to get woe like the wicked, but to go into the chamber. Some scholars interpret the chamber as the Goshen land, and the others signify the rapture, but both have a common point in avoiding the tribulation of the Jehovah. When you see Jerusalem besieged, Jesus told us to flee to the mountains. (Luke 21: 20-21)

In Zephaniah 2:3, it says that keep all the ordinances of the LORD, all of you humble, seek the LORD and seek justice and humility. It is written that you will be hidden in the day of the Lord's anger. The term 'hidden' is the

---

same meaning as that of David being hidden from Saul, or Elijah was hidden from evil queen Isabel by God. At the end of time, the believers of God suffer persecution and martyrdom from the forces of the evil Antichrist, but some will be hidden. All believers are not necessarily martyred. To be martyred is up to the Lord's will, and the weak ones to crumble by torture may be hidden in advance. God will use it according to the one's capacity.

In Psalm 27:5, it is written that the LORD shall keep me in his pavilion in the time of trouble, and his tabernacle will hide me in the secret place, and he will set me upon a rock. The author of the Psalm also said that on the day of trouble, God hid in his pavilion or tabernacle. There have been many tribulations in King David's life. However, God says that he kept David in his tabernacle.

Joel 2:32 says that there will be someone to escape from Jerusalem on the day of trouble. Before the great and terrible days of Jehovah, the sun will be darkened, and the moon will be turned like blood, as it will happen in the trumpet disaster (fourth). The trumpet disaster is a day of trouble; the last trumpet in 1 Corinthians 15:51 is the seventh trumpet. At the moment of blowing the seventh trumpet, it suddenly changes and is lifted into the air. Only the last trumpet will overcome the power of death, and the believers will finally be resurrected. In verse 57, it says that God will give us the victory through our Lord Jesus Christ. The rapture is the occasion when Jesus meets the Bridegroom who changed into the holy body on white raiment.

White raiment was said to be sacred works of believers. When they are being raptured, it changes in an instant, into white raiment. The old clothes that were worn will fall on the floor. When Elijah ascended, his outer garment fell from the sky. When Jesus was resurrected, the linen cloth that wrapped Jesus lay in the tomb. The luxury clothes we wear on the flesh cannot eventually be taken to heaven. In the name of Jesus, when the righteous act of repentance and word is done every day, the white raiment of the believers are cleansed. (Revelation 19:8) White raiment is the robes for the believers to wear when they participate in the marriage supper of the Lamb. A man without the robe can never be the bride of the Lord. Those who cannot clean the raiment will eventually be left on the earth and pass the Great Tribulation. There are places to run away and hide in God's grace to those who are left behind. The Bible repeatedly communicates these messages to those who pray through the Holy Spirit.

Enoch's Rapture (Rapture before Tranquility)	Features	Rapture without tribulation, first fruit raptured by small-scale gentiles.
	Time	During the Pre three and a half year, after the sixth seal opened.
The Rapture of Elijah (Rapture during the Tribulation)	Features	The rapture during the tribulation, the rapture of two witnesses, a hundred and forty-four thousand, the rapture of many Gentiles
	Time	End of the Pre three and a half year, after the seventh trumpet was called
Left Behind	Features	It is left without rapture. Jews and Gentiles fighting without receiving the mark of the beast
	Time	During the Post three and a half years, get through the vial disasters.

The first Rapture
Before the Tribulation

In Revelation chapter 6, there is a severe earthquake after the sixth seal is taken away, and the sun is darkened like mourning woven with black fur, and the moon is like blood, and the stars fall on the earth, even as a fig tree fell on the mighty wind. The heavens drift away as the scroll drifts, and the mountains and the islands are removed from their place, and the kings of the earth, the royal families, the generals, the rich, the strong, and all the servants and freemen hide in the dens and rocks of the mountains. It is happening after the continuously great events of the sixth seal opened, a hundred and forty-four thousand of Israel's get sealed on the forehead which will be redeemed later. The apostle John recorded several specific tribes. This record is equal to the number of tribal wars in numbers. However, Joseph and Levi's tribes are included instead of the tribe of Ephraim and the Dan.

Twelve thousand of each tribe are supposed to serve as the first fruit of the Jewish people. The first fruit is belonging to God and must harvest before it is ripened. The remainder of the fruits will bloom on the branches. If you do not crop, all the nutrients will go to the first fruit, and the remaining fruits will not grow well. A hundred and forty-four thousand of the sons of Israel, who became the first fruit, ministered with two witnesses. They were raptured after the seventh trumpet was called. Their rapture event is the moment when the Jews accepted Jesus as the Messiah.

On the other hand, the fruit for the salvation of the Gentiles is told in Revelation 7:9. "After this, they come out of their nations, and in their families, and the people, and in the tongues, and are dressed in white, and stand before the Lamb." The character of these in white robes is the ones who come out of great tribulation, who are before the throne of God, with a tabernacle on them, no hunger, no thirst, no hurt, and no shedding tears.

Those in white do not exist in the world. These are the ones who washed and whitened their clothes on the blood of the Lamb. These are the Gentiles who have already been martyred or sanctified in the name of Jesus. Moreover, they become the first fruit which has a significant influence on the rapture of the remaining Gentiles. I call this 'the rapture of Enoch' who was raptured before the tribulation. Jesus has left twelve lunchboxes and seven baskets after he has caused the miracle of the five loaves and two fishes, seven loaves and two fishes. It was a miracle for the Jews and a miracle for the Gentiles. He left only twelve lunchboxes after the miracle for the Jews, but he left seven baskets in miracles for the Gentiles. The twelve lunchboxes for the Jews were a small quantity. However, the term 'basket' is a large one that is used for carrying significant size materials or carrying people. The secret explains that the Gentiles were grafted in the olive tree and bear fruits.

Timeline of the first rapture	A hundred and forty-four thousand Sealed (not immediately raptured but later guaranteed)
	After a while, the first fruit of the Gentiles will be raptured (the rapture of the Gentiles causes the church to wake up and bear fruits)
	Time: After a sixth of seal opened, during the pre-three and a half years tribulation

The second Rapture During the Tribulation

The book of Revelation must be interpreted literally first. Secondly, it must be explained in chronological order. The symbol is interpreted mostly by the angel to the apostle John. The most parts that angels have not understood are already mentioned in the Old Testament prophets. If you over-interpret the symbols of the book of Revelation, you will fall into heresy, or you will never get the right interpretation. Revelation begins with the reproofs and precepts of the seven churches, chapters 1 through 3. Chapters 4 through 19 are arranged in chronological order. As proof of that, the Hebrew word 'Meta' comes out repeatedly in every chapter. 'Meta' means an incident that happened after the previous incident. It is the same word as 'after' in English. Meta continues from Revelation 4:1 to 19:1.

The explanatory chapters in the middle of each section are to be more specific at the same time. The representative Hebrew word 'Kai.' It means the conjunction before and after which is like 'and' in English. The explanatory chapters are Revelation chapter 5, 6, and 7. From chapter 8, you can connect to 10 chronologically. In chapter 11, two witnesses enter the critical section at the same time. Because the last trumpet of the seventh angel is an essential concept, the book of Revelation explains in detail. In the Bible, the two witnesses were anointed prophets and churches to work in the pre-three-and-a-half-year tribulation. The ministries of the two witnesses are to be killed by the Antichrist to appear in chapter 13 and to rise again on their feet on the third day. The case of two witnesses dying in Jerusalem left on the hills of Golgotha, and resurrected in three days will have a significant impact on Israel.

Since the ministry of the two witnesses, there will be 144,000 martyrs to come out. Because of their martyrdom and resurrection, repentance begins throughout Israel, and a resistance movement against the Antichrist occurs. Chapters 12 and 13 are explaining these details. Chapter 14 is about the martyrdom and resurrection of a hundred and forty-four thousand and the big harvest by the angels. When the angels lift the sickle, and the big harvest occurs, the great gentiles will be raptured. When the seventh trumpet, the last trumpet, is called, at first a hundred and forty-four thousand Jews will be raptured, and angels will lift the rest of the Gentiles. Jews and Gentiles who have not been elevated are hidden in the land of Goshen as the remaining descendants of the woman in chapter 12. There you will be nurtured for three and a half years. Revelation is writing in this straightforward way. The Bible is not a difficult book, and it is clear and easy to explain. It is because you have not seen the Old Testament that the Bible feels difficult. There is the New Testament in the Old Testament, Leviticus in the New Testament, and in Jesus Christ, the Leviticus becomes the flesh.

Revelation 15:5 says that there will be a tabernacle of testimony in heaven after these events have occurred. In the tabernacle of the testimony, the angels carry seven vials. The vial disaster occurs after the seventh trumpet is called. The accident happens in order of the seal, trumpet and the vial. From chapter 16, the disaster of vial comes down in order. A vial disaster takes place for forty-two months which is the same period for the Beast; the antichrist that came from the sea to hold power to work.

The Forty-two months period, when the two witnesses die and the two beasts start working, are the same as the three-and-a-half-year period of the great tribulation. The midst of seven- year covenant is the end of the pre-three and a half year and the beginning of post three and a half years. At the middle of the covenant, which Jesus had spoken, he said that the abomination of desolation would enter the holy place.

At this time the second beast will set up an idol in the third temple to worship the first beast. During the seven-year tribulation, the army of the beast has abolished temple sacrifices, surrounding Jerusalem, and waging war against two witnesses and a hundred and forty-four thousand mighty warriors. Currently, Jesus asks those who live in Jerusalem and those living in the city to flee to the mountains or into the wilderness. Daniel chapter 12 and Matthew chapter 24 have written explicitly in details for the words of Revelation chapter 13. A detailed prophecy of the beast is written in the book of Daniel. Jesus tells the reader to understand what is written in Daniel. Some say don't read the Daniel because that the Old Testament was already fulfilled a prophecy. However, Jesus says to read and understand the Old Testament from Daniel. (Matthew 24:15) The beast and those who are left must pass through life, death, and catastrophe for forty-two months. It is what will happen in the future.

After the seventh catastrophic vial disaster in chapter 17, we go over to chapter 18:1. In chapter 17, there is a case that the beast and the whore hate and kill each other. Eventually in chapter 18 Babylon the great and the mother of all abominations the whore falls. She is a world religion, a Babylonian religion that has corrupted all politicians and religious people. Babylonian religion is a gigantic hybrid world religion that collects all idols and abominable demons and corrupts Christianity. Many Christian denominations are joining this religion, and it is time for apostasy. In Revelation 18:4, our Lord commands the believers of these churches to come out from there. The modern Babylonian religion begins with the WCC (World Council of Churches) and turns into a vast world religion. The characteristic of Babylonian religion is to support pluralism, polytheism, and homosexuals.

In Revelation chapter 19, Jesus, who has finished the marriage supper of the Lamb, returns to the earth with his bride. The army of the beast is destroyed and becomes the food of all birds. Ezekiel prophesies that Israel will become a priesthood in the millennial kingdom. At that time all nations must go to Jerusalem to keep the feast of tabernacles. God's feast did not fall on the ground. When the millennial kingdom comes, the Holy Temple is built again. The circumcision system is resurrected again. Gentiles who are not circumcised in their hearts and bodies cannot enter the Temple. There will be the burnt offerings and the sacrifice of thanksgiving to the temple. The Sabbath, the year of rest unto the land and the Jubilee will be kept in full. During the Millennium, humankind will again rehearse into the New Jerusalem. The resurrection of temples, feasts, and ceremonies is to reintroduce Jesus for the descendants of the millennial kingdom. Our Gentile churches must go back to the Bible. The Bible must be read and taught holistically from Genesis to Revelation.

Just as Jesus rejected the useless inheritance of the elders of Israel, the unbiblical traditions of the Gentile churches must be removed like Passover yeast. Now, as Gentiles and Jews become one, we must become one new man and make peace. (Ephesians 2:15) The Gentiles should teach the Messiah for the Jews, and the Jews should teach the Torah for the Gentiles. The rich Gentiles should help the poor Jews. All the words of tithing in Leviticus chapter 27 and Deuteronomy chapter 26 must be obediently kept, and then you should be blessed. The self-proclaimed Jews are wealthy, but the Holy Jews who believe in Jesus are poor people. The believers, among the Gentiles, who have stewardship of the riches, are the will of God to help the poor Jews. To become a steward of wealth, we must receive the blessing of opening the heavenly gates. When the heavens are opened, tens of millions to billions of dollars of wealth are poured out.

In the last days, God is looking for a faithful and wise servant to share his wealth in due season. The steward of the riches is not made by his power but is a person who has accumulated tremendous wealth because God has poured out completely. The stewards of riches are those who live according to the word, and even those who leave their lives to God. The stewards of the wealth must be awakened, not to fall asleep, and always think that the Master, the Lord will come soon. In the last days, stewards of riches prepare their harvest and reserve their strength for the war and tribulation. They must prepare for future conflicts, the world economic panic, and famine, powerful defensive weapons, provisions, and bottled water for the kingdom of God.

In the last days, the stewards of the riches must help Israel to fight the forces of the Antichrist. Christian country and Israel must maintain their strongest alliance and pray daily for peace in Jerusalem. They will invest a lot in human, material and spiritual exchanges between Israel and Christian country. We also need to support politicians who love God's law in the National Assembly and actively cooperate with them to root out homosexuals from this land. Because of the wicked people, the earth is cursed and rotten. The stewards must actively support the righteous so that the ground can be blessed and alive. We should also try to make the Christian country become the land of Goshen at the last time. The stewards of the riches must know that after the rapture all your wealth will be gone. Just as Manna, which covered the wilderness, was gone away when they enter the land of Canaan.

Timeline of the Second rapture	Two witnesses and a hundred and forty-four thousand Jews are raptured
	After that many Gentiles are raptured
	Time: Ending of the pre-three and a half year, after the seventh trumpet was called

Then you shall see and be glad, and flow together,

and your heart shall fear, and be enlarged;

because the abundance of the sea shall be converted

unto you, the forces of the Gentiles shall come unto you.

- Isaiah 60: 5

Part III

"Believer, Remnant and Survivor"

And it shall come to pass, that in all the land,

says the Lord, two parts therein

shall be cut off and die,

but the third shall be left therein

-Zechariah 13:8

The left behind 'Believer.'

There are three classes of people left behind. The first class is those who believe in Jesus and attend church but are not raptured. No matter how long you go to church, you will not qualify if you are not dressed as a bride and continue to wear dirty clothes. The clothes that are worthy of the bride are in the heart that struggles to live according to the holy conduct and the word. The bride should be awake to fill the lamp with oil while the groom is waiting behind the door and being able to leave at any time. Because the bridegroom is slow, the bride who falls asleep can never go with the bridegroom. Some brides love of their wealth and honor. Therefore, they want bridegroom to come a little slower. Such people can never be brides of the bridegroom. Those who steal money to offer church gifts and tithe, and those who lie for their benefit every time, cannot be the brides.

Those who serve in the church and who oversees the office, drunken all the time cannot be the brides. Those who repented by believing in Jesus, but commit stealing, robbery, and murder repeatedly, are not repented truly. It is a terrible sin to abuse the finances of the church and use money as hobby and living expenses. When people commit a trespass, and sin unwittingly in the church thing, God told them to give a trespass offering.

A trespass offering is that you can easily compensate your wrongdoing by adding 20% on the amount of your mistake for forgiveness. However, if you deliberately trespass the church's finances or steal it, it is a death penalty. The church should collect the tithes from the believers and use them according to the tithing ordinances of Leviticus and Deuteronomy. The believers have made an offering to God, and the Church must use it as God's will and his word. If the church has robbed the tithe of God, the church must be cursed. The church will always have a lack of finances and wealth in the barns.

Believers are also obliged to make a worthy investment in their talents and offer them to a beautiful church that has many fruits. There is no fruit in the offerings that are presented to churches that are not beautiful to God. Will the Lord commend the servant who has invested five talents and has not left any profit? We shall give tithes to beautiful fruit-bearing churches and serve there to make more profits for God. If you think that "God is the creator, so he can find and use the money as he wishes, so I can give tithes to anywhere like an evil church." Then you will be blamed. In the Bible, Jesus said. "This evil and lazy servant! Go away from me!" It is a terrible word. The officers of the church who steal offerings must be left behind.

There are those who have spent a long time in church but still have a lukewarm faith. These classes must experience the Holy Spirit and be born again. There is no one to see Jesus without being born again. Even after receiving the eldership or deaconship, those who have a selfish faith like a child will be left behind. These people have been hiding for the past three and a half years of tribulation, becoming mature as well as word and prayer, suffering and sacrifice. Although someone has been in church for a long time, those who always pretend to be noble and selfish without any zeal or obedience will be left behind. They will mature by fasting and starvation in the mountains. Those who are arrogant and proud will remain. They will be hiding in the mountains, and seeing the vial disaster pour out, they will fear God. Hail like a soccer ball and a burning meteor pouring down from the sky. When the sun gets hotter and burns everything, and the sea becomes blood, you will understand that God is so fearful.

Those who will be left among the most believers may be pastors or shepherds. God demanded a higher level of holiness to them. However, they only have enjoyed all things and received respect in a higher place and left behind by the sins of not living according to the Word. Because they have already obtained all their rewards on the earth, they may even reject entitled to enter the city of heaven. Some famous evangelists led the revival assembly for three days and received ten thousand dollars as a lecturer. He/she accepts a luxury meal and luxurious treatment in a hotel as a matter of course. He/she has already taken all his rewards. Not like him/her, those who give their lives for the gospel by themselves will become the first fruit.

In the Bible, God told us to use the offerings as the maintenance of the temple, the living expenses of the Levites, and for the priests. After then God wants us to use offerings to serve the poor, the difficult widows, the orphans, and the strangers. If you buy a private apartment and a good car with God's offering, and use it for your children's tuition, it is robbery. The Levites were supposed to live in tithing. It is about the cost of living for the average Jewish family. If the church is so abundant that the money overflows, it means the church must help other difficult churches. If you know a pastor who is in financial difficulty or a sick church member who need surgery, help them.

Some pastors secretly conceal the offerings of the believers and pretend to build churches in the mission fields. They take a few pictures of buildings and introduce it as churches they have made and deceive the church members. In foreign missions, there is about half the number of false missionaries depending on the region. About 80% of North Korean missionaries are likely to be faked. It is a report of a mission's organization that kept North Korea ministry for a long time. Because North Korea is a particular area with limited information, it is full of a con artist. False missionary reports with fake details deceive the innocent believers and devote their precious gifts to the goats. The church I attended was once fooled by a false North Korean missionary, who nearly took away tens of thousands of valuable for missions but later we kept the value from them. The entire hireling shepherds who are a missionary for money will be left behind.

It is not right for Christians who have businesses to take advantage of deceit or lies. Those who run a jeweler's shop and a restaurant should not deceive the balance. Even if you lose a little, you must run a business honestly. Christian people in the industry who have grown into big corporations should not lose their first intention. I see many Christian businesspeople deteriorating later. When the company is in trouble, they are fasting and devoting to prayer, but if the enterprise rises again, then they fall into the temptation to drink and obscenity again. Entrepreneurs in this way will be left with no matter how much money they donate. After left behind, they will learn about honesty and sincerity for three and a half years. Believers who abuse children will be condemned. A believer who uses violence against their wives and children are also doomed. If you are attending early morning prayer, but your life is not holy, you must think about you become a hypocrite.

Those who are left behinds among the believers are those who have not yet become fruitful. They are those who are unfamiliar with God's word and prayer. There is a plan that God will make them like pure gold through the fiery trial. This is because of God's goodness and kindness. Those who are left should not blame God even if they cannot join the rapture. Instead, we must repent our failure to live according to the Holy Scripture.

Those who are left are those who have not received the mark of the beast. The mark of the beast will be enforced at the beginning of post three and a half year's tribulation period. They are shocked when they see the raptures. Those who are left will seriously worry whether they will get the mark of the beast or escape to the mountains. Then they would abandon all their wealth, honor and possessions and run away to the mountains. In conclusion, they will be victorious without receiving the mark of the beast.

According to the denomination, some churches receive the mark of the beast. These churches will receive the mark of the beast after pre-three and a half year of tribulation. However, their peace is brief. When the first vial is poured out, those who receive the mark of the beast suffer by a noisome and grievous sore upon the area. Churches that accept the mark of the beast do not believe in the rapture. They think that aliens massively abduct the rapture. To prevent kidnapping, control chips that are planted on human bodies are more persuasive. Those who have not received the mark of the beast are prohibited from trading. They cannot take a shower because they are in the mountains and expecting toilet paper in the bathroom is a luxury. If they are hungry, they should eat snakes or dry insects. It will be beyond their imagination. However, this is much better than torture that is caught in the beast's army and cuts flesh and heat fingers with the fire. The church members who receive the mark of the beast by mistake have time to take it out with a knife until the first vial is poured out. If they pass that time, even their salvation will become blurred because their names will be erased from the book of life.

The mark of the beast is not an absolute symbol. As the apostle John wrote, it must be real and interpreted literally. The mark of the beast is a tool for worship, and for opponents, it is a means of controlling buy or sell. As a means of control, it is to plant things in the form of computer chips in the hands or on the forehead. Some people can question why it is such a big deal with a tiny computer chip. So, let me give you an example. There is a small computer chip called CCD on the mobile phone. This chip can reproduce all the light of the world we see into digital signals and display it on LCD. The CCD has about one-tenth the size of a little fingernail. It transforms all analog light and form existing in the world into tens of thousands of digital colors. Do you believe a single chip has this capability? We use mobile phones efficiently, but we do not know that there are such small chips. The mark of the beast is made of a biomedical semiconductor, and it has traceability, electronic money function and various medical functions of a human being. With a single chip, humans can be given the same bizarre ability as God. Therefore, we call the mark of the beast is the second fruit of the Tree of Knowledge.

During the trumpet disaster, there will be those who are left go against the temptation of the mark of the beast and go into the wilderness to meet God. They are those who have realized that all who have already ascended to the rapture were faithful. Many of them have experienced watching their own family or children to be raptured. Elisha saw Elijah ascend so. At the moment of rapture, people get suddenly changed and dragged into the air. It is like Jesus' disciples saw him ascending into the air and disappeared. Jesus left these words to his disciples before he went up in the air. These signs will follow the believers, and they will cast out evil spirits in my name, speaking new tongues, and picking up serpents by hand. No matter what poison they drink will not be harmed, and they will be healed if they lay their hands on the sick. (Mark 16: 17,18) Those who are left will understand and live by this word.

The new tongues of verse 17 in the Greek word are 'kainos glo:ssa.' This word means that it is a new dialect qualitatively different from what has existed so far. 'Glo:ssa' is interpreted as a human language or race, but in this case, it refers to the dialect used in prayer. All the 'Glo:ssa' that the Apostle Paul spokes are interpreted as "speaking in tongue." It is not a sign of faith in Jesus as we speak a new foreign language. It is because those who do not believe in Jesus can also speak a foreign language. However, only those who believe in Jesus can speak the tongues of the Holy Spirit. The tongue of the Holy Spirit is the language of the angel, and our spirit uses the human tongue to pray. Often important things come to mind while praying in tongues. At that time, we must also pray with the heart. Then the spiritual prayer and the prayer of the heart each bear fruits. (1 Corinthians 14: 14-15)

Those who are left will receive power by doing the prayer and praise with the fire of the Holy Spirit.

Like Elisha, you gain a double portion of power, a supernatural experience and seek God's help. Life will be uncomfortable for the first few months, but after that, you will feel that your life is more valuable and happier. Those who are left will praise God, by seeing that the disaster of vials avoids their residence. They are the ones who will cry and rejoice the most when Jesus returns. Also, the flesh will change little by little and will live long, praising God with many children. Like Abraham, they will enjoy the blessing of having many offspring. Those who are left will make their precious experiences into books and movies and train for future generations to be born. They should live with the faith that they have experienced to their descendants as a tradition of grandchildren. Therefore, believers are left behind.

A person called 'Remnant.'

The second left behind category is the ones who will be called. Someone who remained in Joel 3:32, would be called by the Lord. A people called by God among the left are leaders who will overcome great tribulation. For example, Enoch went up into heaven, but Noah was called among the remnant. With Noah, humankind could flourish again. His descendant, Jacob, was a man who had suffered for all his life. He is an antitype of a remnant that will pass through tribulation. Joseph, the son of Jacob, is a person whom God has prepared.

Joseph was a remnant who was called by God. He becomes a leader who has been called beforehand among those left behind. Because of Joseph, the family of Jacob went into the land of Goshen and received the reliable protection of God. Joshua, the descendant of Jacob, is also remnant of the calling. Joshua is left behind for the rest of the Canaanite war. However, he could not keep the word of God in full and nor finish the Canaanite war. Through the days of chaos, King David wanted to end the conquest war that Joshua could not complete, but he also broke the word of God and made a peace treaty with the Gentiles. His son Solomon completely disregarded God's Word and ruled, unlike the beginning. Because of this, Israel is cursed and divided into South and North. Because of the rebellion of the kings of North Israel, the earth will be cursed, famine, war, and tribulation.

Elijah was a prophet called to the Northern kingdom of Israel. His ministry was to anoint King Jehu (meaning Judge of God) for the removal of the wickedness of King Ahab and Jezebel in Northern kingdom of Israel. His disciple Elisha becomes a remnant who is called to finish all that he has not done after the ascension of Elijah as Jehu removed the descendants of the king of Ahab and Jezebel as Elijah prophesied. Although Jehu was not a good king, he fulfilled the will of God and received the covenant that the dynasty would last for four generations. However, after Elisha's death, the Northern Kingdom of Israel will quickly fall again. The Southern Kingdom of Judas is also prophesied by the prophet Isaiah due to the mistake of King Hezekiah to be reprimanded and dragged to Babylon. First, the Northern Kingdom of Israel collapsed by mighty Assyria, and powerful Babylon, like a lion, invades Southern kingdom of Judas after capturing Assyria. Nebuchadnezzar, the king of Babylon, stripped off the eyes of Zedekiah, the king of Southern kingdom of Judas. He was naked, and tied with a brass chain, then walked to Babylon with barefoot.

The Israelites, who were taken to Babylon, are mobilized to build the castle walls but are nourished by the river of Chebar. The River Chebar is like the land of Goshen where God protected the Jews since the Babylonian captivity. Ezra is the most representative of those who have been called by God. Ezra was one of the Israelites who was taken to Babylon, the most law-abiding and loving of God's word. God restored the word that had fallen through Ezra and made it possible to rebuild the city of Jerusalem. Also, every week on the synagogue, the Word was proclaimed on the Sabbath. Besides, the words of the Israelites are read by Ezra, and the nation struggles not to re-establish the sin of idolatry.

Daniel, Ezra, Nehemiah, and Zerubbabel come out of Babylon. Tribulation is an excellent place to train people. Those who are left in the tribulation that will arise in the future will receive training of fire and will have faith like pure gold. Many pastors will be left to serve them. Although there is no church building and food is lacking, they will receive supernatural power. The fellowship with God will be restored. They will study prayers and God's words for three and a half years. The pastors who are left should give their lives for the believers. For the sheep that are left, the shepherd must keep them for his own life.

When the time came, Jesus, the Messiah, came to this earth. He came not to judge and rule, but to deliver the Word, the sword. Jesus raised his disciples during the public life, resurrected in three days after the cross, and gave special training for forty days, and ascended into heaven. The apostles left behind call on many of their disciples. Rome has destroyed the holy city of Jerusalem, but those who are called by God preserves the Word. After the fall of Jerusalem, Jesus' disciples spread the gospel to Samaria and the ends of the earth. Many of them will become martyrs during persecution, and the believers will be left in tribulation.

God continues to send those who are called for these

remnants. They suffer from confusion and pain, but God has mercy on the remnant and prepares these workers. The woman in Revelation chapter 12 will have the same role as the underground church during the three and a half years for great tribulation that will occur in the future. The woman conceives, protects and nurtures the believers. The land she will hide behind is called Goshen. The Goshen land will be covered details in the next chapter. God has not just forsaken the left. Do not forget that there is a plan of salvation for those who are left behind. Our God is good, merciful and wants to train those believers to use them as a hero. Just as the Jews were taken to Babylon in the past, but the great men of God have been nurtured.

Unlike the other apostles, the Apostle John had to live for a long time. He had to house his aunt Maria until the death and live for the church of Ephesus, and the first left behind churches. With the teachings of the apostle John, the early church learns the gospel of John and receives John Epistles and the Revelation. Revelation is a message of comfort for all the believers who have been tortured. All the prophecies in Revelation prophesy that the victory of our Lord Jesus Christ and his brides will live and rule the world for a thousand years.

The believers are not dead if they die, but they are

promised through the Revelation that they live forever if they live. No one will receive such a strong message and fail to pass the tribulation. Their enemies catch some, thrown into prison, tested and martyred. However, they also overcome because of the word of the Apostle John. The remnant pastors will take care of the remaining sheep like John the Apostle. Pastors who have lived as hireling shepherds receive the mark of the beast and have eternal death or opportunity to repent once. The hireling ministers who cannot be raptured must repent to death before God so their soul can survive. The hireling ministers will be beaten, spat and mocked by the left goats. They are responsible for the many dirty works they have done in the name of Jesus.

Those who rob the tithe of the Church, steal the precious gifts of the believers, commit adultery with the church member or the whore, do not study the God's word but playing golf all the time. Those who are interested only in church politics, use of violence to their wife and children, set church members differently according to their possessions, and those who sell the church to heretics are typical hireling ministers. If they receive the mark of the beast without repentance, they will be sentenced to the deadly punishment at the judgment in front of the White Throne. It is the Word of God. Revelation 18:4 says that the believers in these churches should come out of there. The members of the Church should not participate in their sins if the church engages in spiritually obscene acts with the WCC. Do not take the plagues they have received.

Please come out from the church of the hireling ministers. Hireling ministers do not teach the Bible in its entirety from Genesis to Revelation and take wrong preaching on the mark of the beast. That will deceive innocent believers. Before the time of Revelation chapter 13 comes, they receive the mark of the beast first. In the age of apostasy, they are the first to spoil Christianity. The church all around the world should not imitate this trend of the West, nor should it cooperate. The church should get out of the wrong theology and faith of the West. Deteriorated truth is no longer pure. We must go back to the Word and live like the early church. Jesus is the one who does not change in the present or the future. Jesus is always the same because he was and has been and will be forever.

Those who have not received the mark of the beast 'Survivor.'

The last group of those left is the unbelievers. Among those who do not believe in Jesus, there are those who do not receive the mark of the beast because of their philosophy and faith. For example, most Jews do not accept the mark of the beast on their hands or forehead. Those who dislike the Antichrist do not receive the mark of the beast. Those who do not receive the benefits of civilization do not accept the mark of the beast. Those who do not go to church but do not receive the mark of the beast will be more in numbers than they think. Satan is only in control of the third part of the earth. Even if he kills people, he has only one-third of authority. When a catastrophe occurs after the rapture, the target is mostly the beast government and his armies. Of course, those who do not believe in Jesus will survive in the mountains, the underworld, and the outback. Jesus said that when the time comes, they must run to the mountains and those in the city must go to the rural. This word applies to those who do not believe.

God wants the unbelievers to survive to the end. When they are alive, they can see Jesus in Revelation chapter 19 who is returning to the earth. As soon as they watch the scene, there will be the tears of repentance and relief in their eyes. Our role is to convey our sincere word to the unbelievers to prepare for the day. If this book is among them, it will help a lot in tribulation. Believers are hiding in the land of Goshen where God has prepared. However, those who do not believe must go into a safe place and survive. The safest places are mountains, caves, wilderness or big islands. The underground is more reliable than the ground. Rock caves in the mountains are also safe. They should also prepare food and water for at least three and a half years. Dried insects, snakes and fruit of plants will be useful. They must acquire drinking water and learn how to use trees, rain, and dew for it.

You must learn various tools and methods for making fire, and you must conceal by camouflage against the enemy's raids or searches. In the case of a trumpet and vial disasters prepare for a big fire, an earthquake, cold, heat, hail, and blood. If the groundwater is contaminated and you cannot drink it, you should purify the dew and rainwater. If all survival abilities have been exhausted, we must sit down on our knees and repent of our sins and accept Jesus as our Savior. On the other hand, there are those who will receive God's supernatural help. It is better to create a few hiding places rather than staying still to increase the chances of survival. The most terrible thing in trouble is men.

There will be someone who will hunt human beings because of lack of food. You must carry weapons to protect yourself and your family. Bow, crossbow, and slingshot, knife, hand ax, expandable baton, and clubs are useful as analog weapons. Weapons that use batteries will become useless. A family of eight or twelve is more likely to survive than a family of four. The minimum number of troops is 10 to 12. You must be one squad to be able to hunt for food and make residence defense. However, if too many people are inhabited, they can be discovered by the drones of the beast army. When you go into the believers' land of Goshen on the move, be sure to ask for help in Jesus' name. There will be a helping hand and a plan of salvation.

The old snake is also a symbol of Satan, but the real snake is a portion of food prepared by God. The fantastic survival of cockroaches is to be human food. The snake digs through the tunnel and collects holes to breathe. You can put smoke into the hole and hunt. Snake is a good stamina food that provides protein to people who will survive for long. If you have hunted wild animals or large animals, you must smoke it or make it dried for keeping long period. When the time comes, the livestock's seeds will dry up, making it difficult to hunt.

On rainy days, rain should be collected using raincoat or vinyl. Rainwater can be stored in jars or dig a hole with vinyl. Plastic cans are good storage space. Antibiotics, ointments and simple surgical tools are needed in case you are sick. If you do not control inflammation, you can lose your life.

When the drones of the beast army rise, you must apply clay to your body. You can hide your body from infrared detection equipment. Military blanket made of aluminum foil can be used versatile. You can warm your body, or you can combine camouflage or sunlight to create a fire. It can receive rainwater, and when it is light and folded, its volume becomes smaller. Also, to avoid seeing where you hide, the tree should be cut and collected as far as possible from the survival area. Salt and stainless-steel cups and lighters are must-have items. Even if you starve for 40 days, there is no problem with survival if you only have salt and water. Salt preserves moisture and slows down weight loss. Stainless steel cups are hygienic and versatile. It can use as a bowl for food, and as well as a cup for drinking water.

When they are hunting animals and eating them, they must peel off their skin, and the blood must be poured into the ground and covered with soil. Because there are many parasites in the blood of an animal, you should never eat it. Especially in the case of a snake, the poison is in the blood, so turn it upside down and leave a drop of water on the ground. Animal skins are versatile and should be well dried and stored. Fur can be used as winter clothing to prepare for cold weather.

Three and a half years before the mark of the beast is

enforced, the earth becomes very cold. At this time, we need winter equipment to beat the strong wind. Fur leather gloves and leather shoes are durable and can be used for a long time. However, after the mark of the beast is forcibly enforced, it will become hot as the whole earth burns for three and a half years. Evacuate in natural caves or underground facilities to avoid the heat. Also, keep the salt well and prepare for this. After much sweat in the heat, when the salt becomes scarce, the body becomes weak quickly. Salt plays a role in maintaining water for life. The believers who keep the Word are like the salt of the church because they keep the church alive.

In Genesis 1:28 God creates man and blesses all lives to grow and multiply. The word of God is eternally valid even after this world is over. Survivors grow and thrive by hiding without receiving the mark of the beast that controls the buy and selling function. Receiving the mark of the beast will be the first to suffer when a vial catastrophe is poured out. It is a tool to idol worship man, not God. If you receive the mark of the beast, you can have the right to trade for life goods, but the beast government controls everything. The last of all those who receive the mark of the beast go to the Lake of fire. On the other hand, those who do not accept the mark of the beast are labeled as potential criminals, but they are blessed. All who have not received the mark of the beast are likely to meet Jesus.

Listen carefully to those who have mistakenly taken the mark of the beast without knowing what exactly it is, or who have realized that the prophecy of the Bible is fulfilled according to the content of this book. You must cut off the mark of the beast immediately strip off with a knife. Because there is GPS on the table of the beast, all the location tracking is possible. Since the mark of the beast is the right tool for worship, it will commit the greatest sin before God. The hologram idol is a sign of the beast, and it grasps the situation of people bowing down and all the cases that come to worship. Even idols speak to humans. There is not much time. Before the first vial is poured out, you must quickly cut off the mark of the beast. Moreover, run away to the wilderness to the mountains. After you have cut off the mark of the beast, you must abandon all your houses and properties. The beast army will come to your home and catch you. Runaway. Cry out to God. Find, get and knock on the door.

Various programs about survival have been recently made. You can find a variety of broadcast programs on TV, YouTube and documentary on Survival. The British Special Forces, SAS survival manual is translated and sold. Broadcasting and books of survival expert Bear Grills are also beneficial. Various methods of survival have been introduced in many countries. There are many documentaries on these topics in addition to "live in the mountains" on the cable channel. It is because of the fear of apocalypse that such a variety of survival programs are popular at home and abroad. Those who do not believe in Jesus use the term "end-to-end." Human beings are spiritual, and they know little by little how the world is flowing. Jesus told the people to flee to the mountains as enemy soldiers surrounded Jerusalem. Jesus did not tell everyone to stay and martyred. There are many messages in these words. I hope those who have ears will hear, and those who have wisdom will understand.

And I will bring the third part through the fire,

and will refine them as silver is refined,

and will try them as gold tried: they shall call on

my name, and I will hear them: I will say,

It is my people: and they shall say, The Lord is my God.

Zechariah 13:9

Part IV

"The land of Goshen"

And I will server in that day the land of Goshen,

in which my people dwell, that no swarms of flies shall be there;

to the end you may know that

I am the Lord in the midst of the earth.

Exodus 8:22

Tribulation of Jacob

Jacob is the only Bible person who has wrestled with God. Jacob had met with the pre-incarnate Jesus and wrestled. As evidence, God called his name Israel, not Jacob. He asks God to bless him until the end and ultimately fulfills his will. Instead of getting a blessing, Jacob hurts a tendon of his buttocks at the joints of his thigh and lives as a lame lifelong. The Israelites do not eat the cords of the buttocks in the bones of the legs of the sheep to commemorate Jacob's suffering. Jacob was blessed directly from God. But looking back on Jacob's life, it was a series of tribulations. Dinah, daughter of Leah, was raped by Shechem, son of Hamor of the Hivite, who was the prince of the country. Because of this, Simeon and Levi, Jacob's sons, killed Shechem for the sister's revenge and killed all the men of Hamor in the city. Because of this, Jacob is exposed to the threats of the Canaanites and the Perizzites for the rest of his life.

Jacob loses his first love Rachel, whom he loved so much, on the way to Ephrath (Bethlehem) from Bethel. Jacob takes the body of Rachel to Bethlehem and sets up a tombstone of tears. Before the pain of sorrow has gone, he hears that his concubine Bilhah and his first-born Reuben sleep together. Jacob's anger against Reuben does not go away until he dies. Jacob prophesies that Reuben will never be superior. Reuben's birthright is later passed on to Judas. Jacob's life is blessed, and he seemed to be productive as his property multiply, but suddenly he heard about the disappearance of Joseph, his most beloved son. Joseph's brothers lie to him, saying that a wild beast killed him, brought his clothes with blood on it. When Jacob heard the news, he mourned for a long time. Therefore, Jacob was 33 years short-lived than his father, Isaac.

Jacob would have made his heart broken by the sorrow of losing his beloved wife and son rather than the joy of being rich. The wealth that Jacob has been working for his life is gradually lost to famine. The sheep die every day because there is no grass in the fields. The food becomes scarce, and the price of food goes up to the ceiling, so even selling the whole property cannot buy foods. Jacob shouts to his hopeless sons "why are you guys just looking at each other and do nothing?" He sends his ten sons to Egypt for food. Benjamin, the youngest, was left in case of an accident. It means that Jacob prepares himself for losing all his ten sons for sending them to Egypt. Jacob experienced an economic collapse that came by famine. And when the sons of Jacob also consumed all the food they brought, they went to Egypt to seek more food. Due to the demand of the prime minister of Egypt (Joseph), this time they would suffer the pain of leaving Benjamin, their youngest beloved, as a hostage in Egypt.

According to Jacob's life, we may question whether he indeed received God's blessing or not. But at God's point of view, Jacob's life is blessed. If it is successful if there are a lot of properties and blessings in one's life, it is only to serve the Mammon (the god of money). It is because the grace of God is not well-being or wealth, but it is obedience to His will. Jesus said the best thing to do is that to sell all your wealth, give it to the poor, and offer your life to the Lord.

One day Jacob's sons brought a golden cart, given by Pharaoh, and took Jacob into Egypt with a large family of seventy. In Genesis 46:4, God tells Jacob not to fear to go into Egypt. Lord promises Jacob's descendants to be a great nation there and come back to Canaan. God prepared Goshen, a good land in the northern part of Egypt, for the sons of Jacob. Goshen was suitable land for grazing, located in the southeast part of the Nile Delta. In the area of Goshen, God fulfills what He promises to Abraham.

God had planned that Jacob's descendants enlarged in the land of Goshen to make them a nation. They have incubated to become a nation under the protection of a powerful kingdom called Egypt. The area of Goshen is where God lives with the children of faith. The real character of Goshen appears during the tribulation in Egypt. When the time had come, God wanted the descendants of Jacob, who lived in the land of Goshen, to return to Canaan. The tool used for this is the persecution of Pharaoh the King of Egypt. Jacob's descendants cry out, and God prepares Moses. When Moses wanted to bring the people of God into Canaan, Pharaoh refused. God allows ten plagues to abolish the power of Egypt and the power of Pharaoh. While ten diseases occur in Egypt, there was no disaster in the land of Goshen.

The last calamity was inevitable even in the land of Goshen; all Jews were saved by putting the blood of the Lamb on the two side posts and the upper door post of the houses. This event is the occasion for the Passover to be made. It tells us that the main character of the Passover is Jesus. Thus, even if the believers were hiding in the land of Goshen for three years, the blood of Jesus would have to be painted on the side and upper doorpost of their hearts. God's angels kill human beings or harvest (rapture). The standard of living and death is the blood of Jesus; the Lamb as it had been slain. Those who reside in the land of Goshen, where God is with them during the three and a half years of tribulation, will be saved from death. However, to receive eternal salvation, we must accept Jesus as our Savior and be faithful and righteous.

When the seal of Revelation is taken away, the whole

world is driven into the crucible of war and the three and a half years of tribulation begins. The cruel Satan's army uses a biochemical weapon to kill many lives. Food production ceases because there is famine on the ground, and it does not rain for three and a half years. The food price in the warehouse goes up to skyrocket, and the money becomes a useless piece of paper. The earth's magnetic field of heaven drifts and various harmful cosmic rays come in, and the sun and the moon seem red like blood. Satellite and power stations have broken down, and private communication equipment such as mobile phones become unusable, and the whole world grows dark. During the pre-three and a half years, the army of Satan has prepared for such a tribulation, so it has stronger military power than opponents.

The mission of Goshen

Your nation must develop a secure defense system to fight against Satan's army. If your nation united with Satan's army and persecuted Christians, it becomes completely hopeless. If your country wants to be the land of Goshen for the people of God, you must stand by the word. There is hope in correcting all systems such as politics, economy, and military with the Word. If your country becomes the land of Goshen, it will survive without difficulty during the seven-year tribulation. Water and food should be kept for seven years to escape during the ordeal. You can create a 'Seven-Year Storage for tribulation' in the country and save it underground. There are numerous underground facilities over the world to avoid military raids. You can also take advantage of natural caves or artificial caves. You can also upgrade your subway or build an underground fort in the ground. If we have food resources like Joseph, your country will not shake. We need to prepare for the war by creating a large pool that can store rainwater throughout the country. It should be developed as strategic groundwater as Hezekiah built an underground waterway.

For the long run, nuclear power plants on the ground should be removed, but atomic fusion power plants must be built underground to prepare the war. We need to secure strategic supplies and legislate a policy to prepare for the seven-year Tribulation. Adolf Hitler secretly arranged World War II. He made an Autobahn for the airfield runway and greatly expanded the car company to create a tank unit. He quietly built a submarine, blocked the English Channel, and quickly captured Europe with an automatic attack machine. Again, these things should not happen to your land. But in the Bible, the prophecy says that there will be more wars. In 2 Kings Chapter 6, Ben-hadad, the king of Syria, siege the land of Samaria, the capital of the northern kingdom of Israel. Samarians are starting to eat their children due to lack of food. With the help of God, Elisha prophesies that the Syrian army will be withdrawn, and food prices will be reasonable again. The land of Samaria is not the land of Goshen, because it has forsaken God and worshiped idols. But the area is kept in the faithful prophet's prayer.

The land of Goshen is where the great Lord servants like Elisha and the people of God are brought together. The area of Goshen is created in the world without being subject to the Beast. During the tribulation period, the United States will be divided and will have different policies for each state. Political conflict will rise, and civil war will take place. Some provinces will play the role of the land of Goshen inhabited by the people of God. The area of Goshen becomes a strong fortress and rock for the remaining people and serves as a military training center.

The land of Goshen has an exemption from tribulation and the help of God. In Revelation chapter 12, a woman takes two wings of a great eagle and flies to a safe place in the wilderness. In the back of the woman, Satan tries to carry her out with the flood-like water comes out of his mouth. However, the earth helped the woman to open its mouth and swallow the river. Satan and Beast attempt to kill the remnant of God hidden in the land of Goshen, but the land protects them. In Exodus 19:4, God says that He led the people of Israel with the eagle wings. The two wings of the eagle express God's strong protection. God protected his people with the pillar of cloud by day, and the pillar of fire by night. And He gave manna every day so that God's people would not starve to death. Wilderness is a dangerous area without a defensive tower or wall. But God has always protected the Israelites with the two big wings of an eagle. The same grace and protection of God will arise in the land of Goshen.

The land of Goshen is not a particular area, but a place where God's people live. If your country plays the role of Goshen, many Christian refugees should be accepted. Your nation must help those who are persecuted and become great refugees. False prophets will deceive the believers and take away their possessions, saying that the land of Goshen is a foreign land. Never be misled by such claims. The area of Goshen must be made in the country where you live.

Living near the sea in the last days can be dangerous. After a major earthquake, tsunamis will hit cities near the sea. Tire, Sidon, and the Philistines were all seaside. The evil forces that shake America's spiritual world are centered on a town near the sea. Israel's Tel Aviv is also one of the evilest cities. An excellent place to meet God will be worth more rather than a brilliant but evil city.

The land of Goshen will be a golden period to prepare end times. Many souls will be harvested, and some time will be given to prepare for the upcoming tribulation. God will provide significant economic support to your country. You must be ready for the good works of God with money and influence. You must fortify your land and place weapons for defense. You must have the ability to develop missiles that can be used by infantry and easily shoot enemy aircraft. The country should form a stable coalition with right Christian Country, not Roman Catholic. It should be made a place of prayer and worship in the country. If prayer places and churches of believers are created throughout the country, your land will become a mighty Goshen.

The country will have a spiritual air defense network due to its prayer place. Each prayer place is connected and will prevent any enemy attacks and natural disasters during the tribulation period. Airplanes and missiles of the enemy will fall on the spiritual air defense network. God's divine shield will be formed around the prayer center and will defend all over the country. Of course, real defense weapons are also needed, but spiritual guards are even more critical. The holy dwelling places and churches will be fortress and rock to escape. The angels of God will protect the believers living in the land of Goshen. If World War III occurs and 200 million people die, you should pray that the damage to your soldiers and civilians will be minimized. Your land must be holy to become the land of Goshen. When people are righteous, the earth is blessed. On the contrary, when people fall, the ground is cursed, and all is lost.

So that your land to be blessed, you must train many holy people. Theological colleges must nurture the sacred disciples. The church must conceive sacred believers. The National Assembly must pass through divine laws and drive out all the lewd and evil forces that curse your land. Those who are economically wealthy should donate their money to the poor and become the light and salt of the world. At the end of time, money will be worthless because the world economy collapses. First, we must put our utmost efforts into securing national food sovereignty. We need to expand the storage period of war materials and stockpile food from three years to seven years and build more food warehouses throughout the country. Overflowing food should be distributed to neighboring countries and refugees. That is the will of God. You should also study how to store rainwater, purify contamination water, and keep food long.

To overcome tribulation wisely, you should be familiar

with analog rather than digital. There is a lot of combat equipment that becomes obsolete when the battery runs out in a military unit. Now, we are living in the digital era, but we need to create a culture to be familiar with analog devices. You must encourage the public to see a lot of paper books, especially reading paper Bible. It is a spiritual strategy for protecting people's frontal lobes from the media and making them wise.

You must understand in advance that all your possessions will disappear over time. Please do not exhaust all your spiritual energies for the property to be rotted. If you seek first for the kingdom of God and his righteousness, then all things shall be added unto you. But receiving more wealth than one's capacity is a curse, not a blessing. It may cause your spiritual death. Do not beg for the help of wealth but ask for the benefits for your country.

Blessed are those who pray for the peace of Israel. God will bless this land while your nation keeps the pro-Israel policy. All the countries that trample on Israel and attempt to divide the ground will disappear from the earth. America was most blessed when it has the most economical and military supports in Israel. On the other hand, America was most cursed, when it had a hostile relationship with Israel. Also, your nation must make the land blessed by opening its pro-Israel policy. Do not be afraid of Arab states and terrorists around Israel. Blessed are the countries that are persecuted for righteousness. Ministers must first be sanctified to restore the authority of the church. It is because; only holy shepherds can nurture holy sheep. Also, laymen should wake up. When the church revives spiritually, it will first be recognized by the neighbors of the region, and furthermore, it will be ready to overcome the tribulation.

The only way for the laymen to become holy is to study the word and follow as it says. We must learn the repetitive message throughout the Bible and the lessons of God. You must read the Bible in its entirety from Genesis to Revelation. There is nothing abolished in the law of God except the sacrifice of the Lamb, the circumcision of the flesh, and the food of righteousness and uncleanness. None of the commandments related to morality and holiness have fallen on the earth and are valid until the end of the world. You must know the Old Testament accurately so you can understand the secrets of the New Testament. You should know that most authors of the New Testament are master the Old Testament. You must read Leviticus and Deuteronomy to understand who God is. In the Gospel of Jesus, he quoted many of the Pentateuch and prophets.

The Apostle Paul was a disciple of Gamaliel, who was one of the Three Great Rabbi. He was a man of the Pentateuch, the prophets, and the Jewish law. Most of the epistles Paul wrote based on this knowledge. To fully understand Paul's epistles, we must study the Pentateuch, history books, and prophets. That's because it is the key to unlock the Word. When the towel that covers our eyes begins to be collected, Jesus will begin to be seen in the Bible.

If we do not understand the book of Daniel, we will never be able to solve the book of Revelation. Numerous symbols in the book of Revelation cannot be deciphered if they are not skilled in the Old Testament. The symbol should no longer be a symbol, but a literal interpretation. The Bible already contains a deciphering method. If you see both the Old and New Testaments and try to keep all the words holy, Jesus will start to be seen.

The essential condition for becoming a holy Goshen is that the Word is raised, and God heals your land. The earth will be blessed when the Word revival movement takes place nationwide, and people are renewed. The selfish life of faith, which is to satisfy only the greed of the self, should now be abandoned. Holy praise must come. You must discard the CCM which songs to show people to their own emotions. We must stop praying and asking for our greed. We must pray to struggle for God's kingdom and righteousness. God commands us to read the whole Bible every seven years. God will be delighted if all the churches and families are going through the seven-year reading Bible movement. If your country aspires to the Word so earnestly, God will also rejoice and bless it. The only way for your country to become dominant is the revival of the Word.

The sons of the Father,

The grandsons of the Father,

Let all the possessions stay in the land of Goshen

and be near to me.

- Genesis 45:10

Part V

"The mark of the Beast"

And he shall confirm the covenant with many for one week:

and in the midst of the week he shall cause the sacrifice and the

oblation to cease, and for the overspreading of abomination, he

shall make it desolate, even until the consummation and that

determined shall be poured upon the desolate.

Daniel 9:27

Who is the Antichrist?

To interpret the book of Revelation, we must look closely at the book of Daniel which is the key to Revelation. The book of Daniel is a detailed account of Babylon. We must know the book of Daniel to understand Babylon the great, which appears in Revelation chapter 16. Daniel chapter 9 and chapter 11 is also called sections of the Antichrist among theologians. The "he" that appears in Daniel chapter 11 is the antichrist. Many theologians interpret "he" as Syrian King Antiochus Epiphanes IV in the history between the Old Testament and the New Testament. He sprinkled swine's blood on the temple and built a statue of Zeus, but he did not become a god. He is weakened by Jewish zealots and easily dies during the war. Antiochus has never built his palace in the sight of the temple mountain and the sea as Daniel mentioned.

Antiochus, like the Roman emperors, can be interpreted as a type of antichrist but not an absolute Antichrist. What Jesus quoted and prophesied about Daniel 9:27 were about what will happen in the future. Some claim that this was the case of General Titus of Rome who destroyed the temple in AD 70 by taking Jerusalem. But Titus did not force his statue into the temple to be worshipped by people all over the world. According to Revelation chapter 13, the image of the beast could speak. However, the speaking image of the beast cannot be made in Roman times. It is a holographic idol to be made in the future and can be made all over the world at the same time

In Daniel chapter 11, "he," which is typified as the Antichrist, says that the palace (headquarters) is built between the sea and the glorious and holy mountain (temple). After attacking and conquering Israel, the Antichrist establishes his bases amid the temple mountain and the sea. His offices will be like a natural fortress. It is headquarters specialized in defense, but he gets angry at the news coming from Northeast. But by the end of the day, no one will be able to help him (Daniel 11:45).

The northern king in Daniel chapter 11 means the army of the Antichrist, and the Southern king is the opposite force. The war between the northern king and the southern king will occur so many during the seven-year tribulation period. In the book of Revelation, there are three great wars during the seven-year tribulation period. It is the war that will happen in the disaster of the seal and the war that will occur in the trumpet disaster. At the time of the catastrophe of the seal, one-quarter of the population will die because of various viruses spread during the war. At the time of the trumpet disaster, some 200 million troops fight each other, and one-third of the population dies.

The last war is the Megiddo war that takes place in the northern plains of the city of Jerusalem during the vial disaster. The northern king began to lose power in earnest after the vial disaster. Among the southern kings, especially the eastern allies oppress the Antichrist forces to be gathered in Megiddo. It is as if Hitler gathered all his armies in Normandy and made it the last fortress. Because the kings of the east will cross the Euphrates River and attempt to advance north of Jerusalem, the Antichrist uses his three filthy spirits to gather the armies of northern kings on Megiddo. The allied forces of the east will fight for their lives and the liberation of Israel. Then a strong command of troops will come from heaven to aid the Oriental Allied Army. Jesus, whom we were so longing for, is returning in the air, riding on a white horse during the war in Megiddo.

The Antichrist is the future leader who will establish a seven-year peace agreement between Israel and the Middle East. And he will allow building the Third Temple. He will be the leader of a vast global government with a coalition of the world's seven strongest allies and the rest of the weak nations. This person will be declared the Messiah by the world's most significant religious leader, like the Pope. A terrorist will kill him with a knife, but he will resurrect in three days. It is his show to get powers from people. The Antichrist will ultimately defeat the enemies and ascend to the Supreme Commander. He forbids the sacrifice of animals in the third temple in Jerusalem and puts his idols in a Holy of Holies. He will persecute and kill the Jews who resist him. He will build a headquarters between the third Temple of Jerusalem and Tel Aviv. If you can see the content of this information on TV or the Internet, you must realize that it is the Antichrist.

Anthropos Arithmos

The mark of the beast in Revelation chapter 13 has been much controversy among theologians. Whether the mark of the beast to consider as a symbol or consider it literally, if you look at the mark of the beast related to salvation, as a symbol rather than a real thing, and if your interpretation is wrong, you will make a fatal irrevocable error. But if you look at the mark of the beast literally, you will be more cautious about salvation.

The mark of the beast in Revelation chapter 13has the following characteristics: The subject who executes to receive a mark is the second beast, a false prophet. A false prophet gets the mark of the beast to worship the first beast, the Antichrist. Here, the original word "mark" is "karagma" in Greek. It means 'sharpen' and 'engrave.' It is to receive a mark in hand or the forehead. It refers to planting in the body using pointed and sharp objects.

The character of the mark of the beast is to kill all those who do not worship idols. North Korea is the most idolatrous country in the world. They think of Kim Il Sung as a sun god. North Korea's Kim Il Sung statue is challenging to search real-time for those who do not worship. It is because it depends on your heart whether you do or do not worship. But the beast's idol can grasp the human mind. It is the mark of the beast that activates the ability. The mark of the beast is an advanced digital device and the number of a man '666'. Number 666 is another name for a computer with digital capabilities. The hologram is digital 666, and the beast is also the digital 666.

'666' is called in Hebrew 'www.' The Internet is digital and the number of a man '666'. For some people, a smartphone can become idols. Many people love the smartphone more than God. They do not feel sorry for God's word, but they are restless for not having a smartphone. The smartphone is like carrying 666. People think that 666 is a bizarre figure with the horns of Satan, but it is digital, the number of a man. The number of a man is the Greek word "Anthropos (man) Arithmos (code)," but it can also be called human-made code. The most significant system created by man is a digital computer.

Computers have also penetrated the human realm. Artificial Intelligence 'Alpha Go' has already won humans in 'baduk,' the domain of infinite humanity. In the future, artificial intelligence will advance into all areas of military, transportation, medicine, economy, and law. All dangerous and difficult works like surgery will be replaced by robots equipped with artificial intelligence. Sooner or later, it will be a world of autonomous vehicles that people do not drive. The era for a human to drive is illegal will come soon. People believe that artificial intelligence is much better than incomplete humans. You must have a special security chip in your body to drive a car, which includes your resident registration and driver's license information in it. If you have the chip with a high degree of encryption, you can ride on a car. The government can move a car with a criminal directly to a nearby police station. Lifelike in movies will happen in the future.

The number of a man 666 serves as a bridge between all machines and humans. For example, people do not have to line up at a department store to buy kinds of stuff.

It is because department stores and people's wallets are connected by the number of a man 666. Scanning machines planted in department stores check people's wallet in real time. The department store does not need a clerk, and customers do not need to line up for payment. Since there is no cash, there is no fear of being robbed, and it is convenient because there is no thick wallet in your pocket. Until the age of Revelation chapter 13 comes, you can carry this wallet on your body in the form of a plastic card. But when the mark of the beast is enforced, it will be planted in the hand or forehead.

The mark of the beast is related to the worship of the beast. The media continues to evolve to worship the beast effectively. In the future, 2D plane images will be converted into 3D hologram images. From this year, VR (Virtual Reality) will become popular. The hologram is the last step of the complete picture that humans can materialize. In Revelation 13:14, a false prophet makes an idol for the beast. Only the hologram is the fastest way to create millions of idols. In chapter 15, just digital technology can provide vitality unto the image of the beast and make it possible to find the person who does not bow to the idol in real time. The holographic idol can track all those who have planted the chip in real time. Hologram idol using laser lights and looks very real and alive to human eyes. Size can be made from several tens of meters to more than one hundred meters. The statue of Kim Il

Sung in North Korea is 23 meters high. The Statue of Liberty is 46 meters high. The height of the beast idols that the false prophet will make is far taller than the Statue of Liberty.

Seven heads and
The ten horns Beast

The mark of the beast is enforced since there was a great rapture throughout the earth. It is shortly after many Jews woke up because there were two witnesses and the resurrection of a hundred and forty-four thousand. The mark of the beast is a vital stone marker that separates pre-three and a half year from post three and a half years. The survivors who escape from the mark of the beast are those who have not participated in the rapture. They will not be able to buy and sell naturally. It is because all credit cards are discarded except in the form of a multifunctional chip where personal information and a bank account are linked. They also lose property and run away to the mountains and wilderness. The problem of food and water shortage will be the biggest issue. There may even be people who starve to death.

The countries in which the mark of the beast is enforced

are all under the influence of false prophets. They must receive the mark of the beast. It tells us that countries have somehow modernized. Underdeveloped countries are not covered. The land of Goshen should be kept from the influence of false prophets. In Israel, the Jews actively resist. Because of the mark of the beasts, the Jews have no choice but to go to war. The land of Goshen should also prepare the war. Even if the false prophets and the army of the beasts come in, the battle must be won by the help of the LORD Almighty.

If your country becomes the land of Goshen, your country must stand alone when the world economic tsunami strikes back. God will give grace to your state that it will stand firm. Numerous underground minerals and energy resources would also be a great help. The gold, food and water supplies will be your powerful weapon. Your country can hold up with Oriental Ally even if the beast government of a powerful seven-nation coalition isolates you.

The seven heads and ten horns beast tell us that there is a coalition of seven powerful nations and ten leaders. The rest of the body is mud which is a union of rabble countries. They will fall and lose power when we cut off their biggest head. The Bible represents the ten horns as ten kings. The kings are state leaders like the president in modern terms. The most magnificent horn among the ten leaders is the Antichrist. Zechariah chapter 1 has a vision of four horns and a blacksmith. The four horns are evil leaders, including the Antichrist, who are the horn that scatters Judah, Israel, and Jerusalem. But the blacksmiths say they help Israel by cutting horns. The mission of a blacksmith is to knock down its horns. The land of Goshen will have the role of cutting all its horns like four blacksmiths.

The beast government is the most powerful nation in the world. But they are a mixture of iron and clay, so they do not get along well. It is active on the surface but weak inside. Some claims that the beast government can be made from Islamic forces, but the Arab states are not able to become the beast because there is no aircraft carrier. It is because the beast government must have a great defense force to cause world wars. Iran and Saudi Arabia have the most reliable military power among the Islamic forces. But their military strength, combined, does not extend to Israel. If Muslims completely dominate the United States, Britain, France, and Germany, there is a possibility, but the odds are tiny.

The beast state will become the second Roman Empire, invading and plundering other nations. The first leader in raising a beast nation is a dragon. The dragon will go forth to conquer and conquer all the wars. But he cannot defeat the power of two witnesses in Israel. The dragon that fails to win both witnesses gives his throne to the Beast. The beast that ascends from the sea is scarier than a dragon. He is cruel and claiming himself to be a Messiah, insulting God of heaven. The beast quickly becomes a leader by taking control of ten-leaders of the great powers. Going against Israel, they kill and persecute many Jews. They go into the temple and abolish the sacrifice and forced to place their idols in the holiest place.

The remnants of the Jews have a fierce battle with the beast army. Jews are traditionally good at fighting. They will win the end of the three and a half years. The land of Goshen should support these Jews in both materially and morally. We must attack the beast army and weaken its military strength before Israel can prepare for a counterattack. We must also provide weapons, food, and resources to the Israeli resistance forces. The beast army will try to kill all the Jews so that the prophecies of Revelation will not be fulfilled. The Bible tells us that the Asian Kings who are never known by Jews will come from the East to help Jews. The leaders of the land of Goshen must have this vision.

For example, North Koreans are experiencing a tribulation. God has given this pain to North Korea in advance for the last days. The people, who have undergone isolationism like North Korea, will cope wisely. The Goshen state must cut off all ties with the beast states since the seven heads, and ten horns nations were created. The Korean Peninsula has prepared a lot of war for the last 70 years, so it will defend well even if the army of the beast strikes. You must defeat the enemy's aircraft carriers, fighters, and fleets at sea and actively resist enemies from stepping on the ground. China will block the enemies that come from on the land. Sadly, many people will die in that fight.

The Goshen state should provide military supports behind allies at all cost. Even if the army of the beast launches nuclear weapons, we must pray for the spiritual air defense system to make the nuclear weapons to fall on its own. There will be prayer places throughout the nation of Goshen that will be the spiritual air defense network. A government that will be seven heads and the ten horns will surely perish according to the prophecies of the book of Revelation. Wise leaders must read and understand the Bible. No matter how terrible and frightening the seven heads and the ten horns beast is, the Goshen state should not be allied with them and should stop trading. We must fear God, who is not afraid of the beast, but who can bring the beast into the Lake of fire to perish forever. Their destruction is already recorded in the Bible. There are foolish and who will die with them. Our people, who became the Goshen state, should never do such silly things.

Dragon is Satan to lead the pre-three and a half years and Beast is the Antichrist called Abaddon who will lead post three and a half years. (Revelation 9:11) A false prophet is the one who will help the beast to be idolized. He looks like a sheep externally, but he is evil with horns. The Goshen state should withdraw from the religious integration movement. Alliance with other religions is idolatry and obscenity. Even if the land of Goshen goes to isolationism, it is blessed if you look only at Jesus and stand on the side of God.

The war of post-three and a half-year is a war between those who have received the mark of the beast and those who have not. During this period, fierce war and environmental disaster will come. The remnant will be strong and wise to overcome these disasters. The allied nations of Korea and China will fight against the beast armies and drive them to Megiddo (Armageddon) in Israel. The beast army sets the last fort and draws the command of the east to it. Megiddo is a broad plain on the north side of Jerusalem, the route to the headquarters of the beast. The beast gathers his forces there for the final war. The army of the east march on Megiddo attacking the beast headquarters to save Israel. Where the command of the east will see Jesus descending from the heaven with the holy army, Jesus comes in a white horse that human beings cannot express, and his clothes are as red as blood. After that, many raptured people will follow after Jesus riding on white horses. The army of the beast blasphemes against Jesus coming down from heaven and shoots all kinds of weapons but does not work at all.

The holy rebuke from Jesus' mouth will sound louder than the thunder and lightning. All the soldiers of the beast army are astonished by the sound, and their hearts will fail. The beast forces are all dead in the place, and the birds of the air fly and eat the dead body. The beast and the false prophet are taken in their area and go straight to the Lake of fire. Satan is trapped in the abyss for a thousand years where the beast was imprisoned before. The abyss is a dungeon under the deep sea of the earth. Angels have the key to an abyss and serve as guardians. Satan waits for a thousand years until the time comes, and once again the world is in confusion. The last war of humankind between the Gog and the Magog is a tribulation for the descendants of those who are left, and after that the judgment of the White throne awaits.

Those who have been left behind in the book of Revelation chapter 12 will be nurtured for three and a half years through a church or belief community expressed as a woman. The woman has two sons, and her first son becomes the first fruit to be raptured. The immature son of the remaining is left with the woman and is matured through the training of fire. The woman was dressed in the sun, with a moon on its feet, and a crown of twelve stars on its head. The woman is first the image of Israel Joseph dreamed about in Genesis chapter 37. The woman is a community of churches that will lead the remnant of Israel. Secondly, she can extend her interpretation to the Gentile church community that will drive the believers. There are many passages in the Bible about the woman in travail.

The woman feeds children and nourishes them with water. The bread and water are all God's Word. If the child is raised in the womb, it suddenly causes labor for the child to get out. The woman experiences pain. The pain is irregularly painful, but there is a period when the pain disappears so that she can rest in the middle. Adjusting the breathing during the pain can withstand the pain enough. Over time, the pain becomes stronger and faster, so the pain comes almost once a minute. Every time there is labor, the mother shouts and pours water and blood from her body. It is called true labor when the pain comes strong.

The false labor is pre-three, and a half-year and the true labor is post-three and a half-year. The false labor is the tribulation, and true labor is the great tribulation. If you persevere on true labor for an extended period, the child will appear suddenly. She is freed from all the pain she has had since she gave birth. She will be the happiest person in the world, tearful of joy and happiness that gave birth to a child. That is the pain of labor. The woman is a community of beliefs in the church that persevered to the end. The church suffers from the pain of labor, but after the suffering, gives birth to a beautiful Son (holy believers).

A woman when she is in travail has sorrow

because her hour comes: but as soon as

she is delivered of the child, she remembers no more

the anguish, for joy that a man is born into the world.

- John 16:21

Part VI

"Tribulation"

Many shall be purified, and made white,

and tried, but the wicked shall do wickedly:

and none of the wicked shall understand;

but the wise shall understand.

-Daniel 12:10

Pre three and half year's tribulation

When the time of Revelation opens, disasters will come for seven years, such as the seal, the trumpet, and the vial. Among them, the sum of the periods of the seal and trumpet disasters are three and a half years. In the meantime, the Great Tribulation does not happen, but a relatively bearable tribulation occurs. At this time believers should sell their possessions and prepare for the end times. Those who live in the city are advised to make for the war or move to the countryside where there are many mountains and trees. It is better for land and a house at the time of peace because an area of the country can be more expensive than a city at this time. Besides, food must be prepared in advance to prevent famine. When a Dragon's army invades your country and takes over the capital, run away to mountains and wilderness. You may need to immigrate to an excellent state to fight to the end against the Dragon's army, or you may have to go into exile.

The high number of the Gentiles is lifted when a hundred and forty-four thousand sealed of Israel are ready. The first rapture has begun. Remnants who have not participated in this rapture are given the opportunity to participate in the second rapture, which will be followed by the large trumpet. The first rapture will involve distinguished holy believers. They have nothing to rebuke in words and actions — those who struggle to live according to the word of God. Unexpectedly many pastors may be excluded from the first rapture. The remnants will lose friends and family because of disaster, war, and famine. There is no electricity, and clean life becomes a luxury. The sun and moon lose strength, and the earth gets cold and colder. Water becomes scarce, and bitter water causes many people to die. A strange locust that has never been seen will make people sick for five months. Every day people die, but they do not repent. Preferably, people are full of malice, worship idols, call demons, murder, fornicate, and steal goods.

While the trumpet disaster is taking place, the world will be entirely divided into sheep and goats, in other words, the children of God and the children of Satan. The children of Satan are sinning even more wickedly. On the other hand, God's people try to repent and live holy. Through tribulation, the possession of God is separated from the property of Satan. Later, the ownership of God is transferred to heaven, but the slaves of Satan fall into the Lake of fire.

Those who remain at the time of the trumpet disaster do not yet receive the mark of the beast. Some countries are subject to extreme persecution, and some are not.

The land of refuge is troubled by global environmental disasters and war but is enduring. A whole third of the world's woods and greenery will burn, and dust and polluted air will bother your nose. You will not be able to eat seafood, and your body will have nutritional deficiencies. Antibiotics and essential medicines will also be difficult to obtain.

Salt and spices will be very expensive. You will not be able to eat like before, and your body will become very poor. Older people, young children, and pregnant women will be especially painful. During this time, two witnesses of Israel and an army of a hundred forty-four thousand will fight against the Dragon and the Beast. However, the two witnesses and their believers are all killed by the Beast army which is more brutal than the dragon. The war will be fierce, and the last person will resist without saving his life. It is finally the day when the whole world is in shock. It is because there will be a great rapture among the nations on the day when the two witnesses and their army are resurrected and lifted to the air on the third day. On that day, the secret of the prophecy will be released. The Beast will drive a massive rapture to the abduction of aliens, but the Jews do not believe in Beast and the media because they have seen themselves with their own eyes.

Post three- and half-year
great tribulation

The remnant Jews will see this fantastic fact and realize the Messiah. After realizing that Jesus is the Messiah, they will resist the Beast and his army, but for three and a half years, Jerusalem will be trampled by the Gentiles. The starting point is just before the first vial is poured. After pre-three and a half year, the great tribulation will take place. At this time, the mark of the beast is imposed by the false prophet, and persecution occurs. States that have been occupied by Beast armies can live if they receive the mark of the beast regardless of their status. The Beast and the false prophet deny God to the end and do not believe in the rapture. Instead, it puts the image of the Beast into the temple and quickly sets up a hologram digital idol in the principal dwelling of the occupied nations. Those who receive the mark of the beast are dulled by the frontal lobe and are more deceived and accept the Beast as the Messiah. On the other hand, the Jews are putting their lives to resist the mark of the beast.

The remaining Jews are prepared to meet the Messiah for three and a half years after receiving the training of fire. During this time, the Beast army is in a terrible war with the Jews. As a result, the Beast army can never defeat the

Jews, because the Jews are with God. They will cry out in search of God. God will answer their prayers and give them a message of restoration. When the Messiah comes down from heaven, the prophet will prophesy again that the Beast army will be wiped out. The Jews will no longer be amazed by their fear. The remnant of the Gentiles should prepare for the disaster of the vial. The vial catastrophe will take place against the Beast army, but it will also have an environmental impact globally. The environmental hazard caused by the disasters of the vial is as follows.

The sea becomes blood, and all creatures die, and the ship cannot quickly move. The source of rivers and water also becomes blood, and you can no longer drink it. The sun becomes many times hotter. The rain will not come, and the burning sun will split all the lands like turtle shells. Many idols worshiped islands and mountains will disappear by earthquakes. Those who are left will suffer from environmental disasters, wars, and famine every day. The trees and forests that provided the shade from the sun can no longer be seen. The food that we got from the wood is no longer available. It will be like the period of hardship that started in North Korea for three years from the year, 1994. At that time, the people peeled all the roots and barks of trees from the forests and had no more food, and about 3 million people starved to death. The ground is so dry that it is even hard to find the dried insects. We must cry out to God when there are no more hopes left. The only salvation is from the LORD, our God. The Messiah of the Old Testament, the Messiah who had come, and the coming Messiah is Jesus. Search for Jesus and knock on the door. The salvation will happen in the tribulation.

Characteristics of the pre-three and a half year	the emergence of dragons, the sealing disaster, the trumpet disaster, World War III, raptur
Characteristics of the post-three and a half years	the appearance of the Beast, the false prophets, the execution of the mark of the beast, the vial disaster, the Megiddo war, the return of Jesus

'Babylon' the God's iron mace

The first half of the Old Testament is the history of Israel before being taken to Babylon. At Mount Sinai, God and the nation of Israel make a covenant of husband and wife. The wife has promised to serve only the husband, obey, and keep his word. For 40 years in the wilderness, the wife was trained to help her husband well. As soon as they entered the land of Canaan where the milk and honey flow, the wife commits adultery with a man other than her husband. Even when the wife commits sodomy with animals, her husband waited patiently for his lewd wife to return. He kept sending prophets and punished her with a rod to wake her up. (Isaiah 10: 5) An adulterous wife betrayed her husband and committed a greater sin. The husband prepares an iron mace for the final withdrawal so that his wife can escape the evil. The mace is Babylon. (Jeremiah 51:20) A mace is a more powerful and deadly tool than a rod. If you are hit by a rod, your arms and legs will break or swell, but when an iron mace hits you, your head will burst, and your arms or legs will fall off. The mace is much more painful than the rod, but it sure helps to wake up.

God prepares the iron mace for the Israelites because it is better to repent and be saved in a state of being broken or weaken. Because of the evil deeds of Israel, the land is cursed. With war, famine, and disaster, many people die, and only 4,600 are taken to Babylon. Jeremiah and Ezekiel say that it is the blessing of the remnant to be taken away. Babylon is the heart of the enemy, but with the grace of God, it is permitted to serve Jehovah, the one God. The Jews are exploited for labor as they reside by the river. In there, they realize how precious and valuable it is to serve God and listen to the Word. Through the Word, they keep the feast of God.

God foretold that the Israelites would be dragged to Babylon for as many as seventy years of sabbatical years they did not obey. But some of the descendants of Rechab and Jeremiah did not go to Babylon. On the other hand, some people have escaped to Egypt and have entirely disappeared from the sword, famine, and plague. (Jeremiah 42:17) Those who were taken to Assyria before they went to Babylon, mixed with ethnic blend policies, disappear with blurred Jewish physical and mental identity. To prevent this, Leviticus lists God's specific orders for Jewish marriage and food. Babylon invaded Assyria and southern kingdom of Judah, destroying them in sequence, and bringing out those who were useful among the people remaining in the southern kingdom of Judah.

The people, who are taken, dwell by the River of Chebar outside the city of Babylon and are mobilized for the construction of the walls. Fortunately, King Nebuchadnezzar of Babylon respects religion and ethnicity and allows Jews living on the River of Chebar to intermarry. It was like the land of Goshen in Egypt, for the Jews. Babylon was serving the sun god Marduk. Nebuchadnezzar made an idol and persecuted the Jews, but God's intervention destroys the tribulation. The Jews left in Babylon are protected by God's help. For seven years Nebuchadnezzar has been in a state of madness, creating a gap in political power. After his death, enemies those who tried to jealous and killed Daniel perish.

Those who were abandoned in Israel had to suffer miserable lives as they were in the lament of Jeremiah. The whole city was bloody and had to hunger every day with poverty and famine. Children who lost parents had to die on the streets because they could not get foods. People killed others or ate flesh for their desires. The earth was cursed and could not bear a single fruit, and the town suffered from all kinds of diseases and plagues. Israel was no longer a land flowing with milk and honey, but a cursed place. The Gentiles in the surrounding area have driven out the Jews and become new owners just as foxes and wolves come into the vineyards to drive their masters away and pretend as they are the masters. God's temple was destroyed entirely and became a pile of garbage. God's glory is no longer in the temple. The Jews left in Israel were violated by the Gentiles and were killed, dragged, suffered, and sold as slaves. Samaria, the former capital of the northern kingdom of Israel, was no longer the land of the Jews. Samaria allows uncircumcised gentiles to pollute the area and make blood mixed with Gentiles.

The Jews would realize God's preciousness and the importance of worship through the pain of losing their country and the loss of the temple. Ezra, the scholar, studied the law books and documents that he has taken secretly. He teaches the prophecies and histories in the word of God. From the time of the Chebar River, the

Jews began to build synagogues instead of temples and learn the law of God in earnest from there. Thus, the Jews distinguish between the only God, and Marduk, the god of Babylon. They no longer confuse the creator God with the god of prosperity like Baal. God took the Jews every seven years in a sabbatical year to read the law, but Moses and Joshua Samuel could not. The Jews who were released from Babylon returned to Jerusalem and gathered together to learn the law. They weep and repent. Babylon was an iron mace that brought destruction to the Jews, but also it was a spiritual blessing.

The great castle of Babylon

At the end of time, Babylon is resurrected in many forms. Theologians argue that it is the Roman Vatican, and some say it is a fallen metropolis. The great castle of Babylon is the Mecca of the world's largest political and heretical religion that corrupts believers. (Revelation 17:2-6) It will deceive the people and serve the idols of the Antichrist. It becomes a tool to divide believers into sheep and goats. The drunk church members in the lewdness abandon God and serve idols. But those who endure to the end can overcome Babylon. The great castle of Babylon will end up with self-destruction.

Babylon in the past has not entirely disappeared but has continued to exist in the head of human history. It is the reason why the head of the golden statue in the book of Daniel in Babylon. Babylon still lives in the next empire, then the next realm, and again in the head of the last great Beast's empire. Babylon still exists at this point in our lives. Babylon is not physically present but is alive in culture, religion, philosophy, music, and the arts.

Those who will be left in the future will increasingly stay in pain. The first to suffer is the war and political repressions. The more idolaters and homosexuals in the world, the more cursed and famine the land will have. Drought and the death of bees will cause tremendous food problems. The terror of Islamic extremists and the conflicts around resources among nations will cause a lot of local battles. The continuing strife around Israel will eventually be demolished. Israel will become more prosperous and stronger, but the Tel Aviv area near the sea will be warned by God. Russia will covet Israel's resources. Russia, Iran, Turkey, Syria, and the Middle East coalition will attack Israel at the same time. Israel will win the war with the help of God in a dead-end situation. On that day there will be a tremendous earthquake in Israel, and a big hail will make the enemy camps into a wasteland. There will be an epidemic in enemy camps, and fire and sulfur are falling from the sky that will make all high-tech weapons into a lump of scrap metal.

Israel will rejoice in the great victory and will cleanse the land for seven months. At this time the first Antichrist, the Dragon, appears. The Dragon is leading the peace agreement between Israel and the Middle East including Russia and attracting worldwide popularity. The Dragon helps build the Third Temple of Israel and gets the support of the Jews. But the Messianic Jews continue to be persecuted by orthodox Jews and Dragon armies. The Temple is rebuilt, and the sacrifice is allowed again. The Orthodox Jews are taken to the festive atmosphere for three and a half years and become deceived by the Dragon. The role of riding on the body of the Dragon is the whore who represented as the great castle of Babylon. The whore misleads the Dragon and the leaders of the world and kills believers. The whore worships the Beast that will come out in the post three and a half years. The false prophet represented as the second Beast comes from the whore.

On the other hand, the Messianic Jews pray for drought for three and a half years in the land of Israel. It is because the prosperity of the nation can cause spiritual darkness. Two witnesses, the leaders of the Messianic Jews, are constantly threatened by the Dragon's army. God protects their lives for the ministry of Two

Witnesses. In the last days, Messianic Jews will put down all their possessions, professions, and honor. They live a community life and always prepare for persecutions.

The world's most popular leader, the Dragon, continues to triumph over a country that disobeys its means of governance. The Dragon illegal all Christian practices and causes the worst repression in human history. The New World Order, which is governed by Dragon, is trying to make Christians fall into corruption with the whore. Christians of the invaded country by Dragon army escape to the mountains and wilderness. This period corresponds to the time of the sealing disaster in the book of Revelation. It is not a great tribulation, but it is a period when you are suffering from fake travail. The fake travail is supposed to withstand. When the Dragon is persecuting Christians, the world economic systems collapse with hyper-inflation. All countries will suffer from severe food shortages. Famine and catastrophe cause the epidemic, and wars will kill many people.

The dragon, under the influence of the whore, turns all responsibility of this famine to Christians, causing an enormous number of believers to be beheaded in the persecuted area. Some areas use a mechanical guillotine to cut the neck; others have a simple laser solution. Blessed are those among Christians who are not tortured but rather beheaded. The rest will go to the wilderness in the mountains and the islands to the outback. A big earthquake strikes where the Dragon reigns and all of them are hidden by rock crevices or underground bunkers. After this, a hundred and forty-four thousand who were sealed in Israel will be filled. The seal in the book of Ezekiel is that the angel put on the forehead to distinguish God's possession. It is the same concept as the seal of Revelation. It is the seal for a human on the forehead to find who is distinguished as the people of God and those who are not. The Beast mimics God's way to put a mark of the beast on the hand or forehead for his possession.

Believers will be consecrated, will lay down many things, and will look only on God. Those who are not raptured will receive training of fire in the wilderness, like the Jews who have been repented and trained by the river of Chebar. The great castle of Babylon will increase homosexuality, idol worship, Christian apostasy, and killing believers in nations and cities. It becomes a mecca of religion worshiping all kinds of nasty demons and witchcraft, reaching out to many countries and destroying cities and people. Believers will escape from these cities and survive in the wilderness. The great castle of Babylon gives great pain and trials to the believers, but it is a great blessing to the end.

When you are in tribulation, and all these things are come upon you, even in the latter days, if you turn to the LORD your God, and shall be obedient unto his voice.

Deuteronomy 4:30

Part VII

"The Crown"

In that day shall the LORD of hosts be for

a crown of glory, and for a diadem of beauty,

unto the residue of his people

- Isaiah 28: 5

A person who became 'stars.'

Before Jews were taken to Babylon, the crown was the king's exclusive property. Only the king and the queen wear the top on their head. The king defeated the enemy and obtained a crown as a spoil. There will be a promised crown to those who persevere to the end and keep the word of God. People who overcome have pledged to be a pillar of the Temple of God. They also said that God carved their name for eternity. They are forever the stars.

There were remnants of Jews in Persia after the Babylonian Captivity. Mordecai is the son of Jair, the descendant of Benjamin. He is an antitype of a person who has been called among the remnant. Mordecai was a man of solid faith and determination. On the other hand, the Persian Prime minister, Haman, is a descendant of the Amalekites who are the enemies of the Jews. He hates Mordecai, who does not bow to him, and plans to kill all the Jews, including the queen Esther. Haman is an antitype of the antichrist who wants to destroy the Jews. Before mentioning Haman, it is necessary to explain the relationship between his ancestor Amalek and the Jews.

In Exodus chapter 17, God commanded Moses to annihilate Amalek. If the Amalekites could not be exterminated, God said that the descendants of the Jews would fight with Amalek in all ages. But Joshua and the Jews did not obey the Words and fail in the Canaanite conquest war. Moreover, the seven tribes of Canaan were not destroyed, and Jerusalem was still conquered by the Jebusite. In keeping with the will of Moses in Deuteronomy, David killed the giants in the war of conquest and occupied the land where God had given him. But David also made peace with Tire and Sidon, the Canaanites, because he could not keep the word of God ultimately. Tire and Sidon were the predominant enemies of David and Solomon, who wrecked the Jews among the spirit and the body. In the end, the Jews were conquered by Babylon, and Persia conquered Babylon later.

Persia was a vast empire that had 127 castles from India to Cush (Ethiopia) by the time. Haman was a descendant of the Amalekites, which Joshua and David did not destroy, and was a noble family that had succeeded in Persia earlier. If Esther's cousin, Mordecai, bowed to Haman and lowered his head, worldly success would have been assured for him. But Mordecai did not bow down to Haman, the descendant of the Amalekites, because he kept the words of his ancestors. Haman is the enemy of the ancestors of Mordecai, and he is still the son of the enemy. From a human perspective, Mordecai is a very inflexible person. But will he look so in God's point of view? Absolutely not.

The wicked Haman plans to make evil laws to kill Mordecai and all the Jews. He intended to kill the Jews in the middle of the day, end of Adar, the last month of the Jewish period, between the 14th and the 15th. Esther's husband, Ahasuerus, does not know Haman's plan and allows the seal of the king according to his request. Like Haman, all the antichrist figures are trying to destroy Jews in common. However, because of the persuasion of Mordecai, the courage of Esther, and the petition of the Jews, Haman's conspiracy becomes a waste. On the day that the Jews were all planned to be slaughtered, Haman and his family were hanging on the pole and exterminated. The Beast and his army that will tear down the believers for post three and a half years will surely perish like Haman.

Esther and Mordecai receive the dearness of King Ahasuerus and rise to the high place of the Persian Empire and become eternal stars in the hearts of the Jews. Mordecai and Esther are antitypes of those who were crowned among those left after the persecution of the Antichrist. The rabbis of Judaism say that they liked Book of Esther best after the Pentateuch. Among those left behind, those who preserve the word of God will receive a crown of stars. Those who survive the Great

Tribulation will become the ancestors of faith in the millennial kingdom. The remnants, such as Noah, Elisha, and Ezra, became stars in the Bible. Those who pass the tribulation and the training of fire will change the world with honorable personality and faith. It is God's good plan for the remnant.

And they that be wise shall shine as the brightness

of the firmament, and they that turn many

to righteousness as the stars Forever and ever.

Daniel 12: 3

Recovery of the Jubilee

The book of Ruth speaks about the tribulation of a family who has left the Word and left Israel. The family of Naomi was cursed in the land of Moab where the Gentiles lived and wasted their possessions. Naomi and her daughter-in-law Ruth follow God's word and go back to Bethlehem in Israel. Naomi, who lost everything, has now realized the word of God. Naomi may have gone back to her hometown, Bethlehem, and thought she might be working for others or begging for a living. Ruth and Naomi symbolize the alliance of Gentiles and

Jews. Ruth acts in obedience to the Word as Naomi says. Naomi's kin Boaz is the one who protects weak, and a poor young woman, Ruth.

Boaz was a mighty man of the Jews and a righteous man of Bethlehem. Boaz was a man who lives according to the word of God. He incurs a loss to marry Ruth because he had to do kinsman's part, and he restores everything for Naomi by paying a high price for the land of Naomi. The spirit of the sabbatical year and the jubilee can be seen through the Boaz. The sabbatical year is a good system for resting the earth and restoring the relationship between the poor, the servants and the rich. Jubilee is like a super sabbatical year concept that follows when the sabbatical year repeats seven times. Everything is rebooting, and it becomes a year of happiness. All the positions of the poor and the servants are back to their original. It is the year when the rich and the powerful will put down their privileges. Ruth, who was poor, married Boaz the mighty, and gave birth to Obed and made the descendants of the royal King David family. The crown of the remnant is to make the lineage of a royal priesthood like Ruth through the millennium. The blood of Jews and Gentiles are spiritually united in Jesus and becomes a people of the millennial kingdom.

When Jesus comes, all the powers and wealth that exist

on earth will return to the original position and the days of joy will continue. It is what the Bible speaks. There has never been a jubilee on the planet. But the kingdom that Jesus governs will be the beginning of the jubilee year and will be kept during the millennium. The beginning of the Jubilee means that capitalism and communism will disappear forever on earth. The Bible speaks of God's Word, history, and economy. Among them, the economic system speaks of tithing and compensation, and sabbatical year and Jubilee. The financial policy in the Bible is aimed at a fair system for the weak. The original owner of the earth belongs to God, and humans borrow it for a while, and they return it at the Jubilee. (Leviticus 25:23) The rich people should not ignore the poor, and God's possession in their property should be given free to those who are hungry. In the jubilee, debts are forgiven, and slaves become free. Jubilee is the complete economic system in the Bible. When the millennial kingdom comes, this word will be fulfilled.

The beginning of healing

The seven vials are God's wrath for the blood and cry of the martyrs. The object of anger is the Beast and his army. All the people in the world who do not believe in God and worship idols are also the object of wrath. In the refuge where believers live, the anger of vials will be avoided. If we remove the idol and homosexuality in the country, your land will become a real refuge. Healing will occur when God's words are raised on earth. Martyrs' sacrifice will sanctify our nation. The Earth's land, its oceans, and its water, which was destroyed by the catastrophe, are restored after the coming of the Messiah. The Ezekiel temple is made, and the water comes from under the eastern threshold of the place heals and repairs the sea. The trees that grow near the water and its fruits will treat humans. Those who remain in the tribulation shall be reminded the message of recovery and persevere to the end.

When the water from the temple heals the sea and the river, the trees planted near the water bring forth the best fruits every month. The leaf of the fruit tree becomes precious medicine materials. Trees and grass grow back on the earth, and the natural ecosystem is recovered. Many fishes will rise in the healing water. The number of fishes is huge by species, so fish resources become abundant. It is excellent news for those who like fresh sushi and various seafood. Animals and plants are restored to their original nature. Huge animals and plants will flood all over the earth. Predators and deadly snakes will become gentle and harmless to humans. Many of the animals and plants just before extinction will be restored, and people will rule them well.

The life expectancy of human beings will increase again. Just as the descendants of Adam and Eve lived, human life would be like a tree. However, this phenomenon will be extended slowly as in the aftermath of Noah's flood. The axis of the earth will be restored, and the four seasons will disappear, and the mild climate will always last. The political and economic systems of the nations will also be stable. The millennial kingdom ruled by Messiah that Jews desired so much for thousands of years is coming. There will be no disputes over all nations and races. Israel is the firstborn of all nations and a priest country. Humanity begins to recover, and many people live on earth. During the Millennium, humans learn the Word of God and practice rehearsals to become people of New Heaven and Earth.

The millennial kingdom is created in this land, our earth, before the New Heaven and New Earth. God gives one more chance on this earth for the descendants of the remaining. Our God is merciful, gracious, slow in anger, and has many good and right things. (Exodus 34:6) He is keeping mercy for a thousand generations and forgiving iniquity and transgression, but still, he is who will by no means clear the guilty; visiting the iniquity of the fathers upon the children and upon the children's children unto the third and to the fourth generation. (Exodus 34:7) In the millennial kingdom, the temple of Ezekiel is created. The sacrifice offering is resurrected again, and the feast of

God is kept. It is returning to the era of the law through the training of living God's word and the practice of being a people of heaven. Till heaven and earth pass, one jot or one tittle shall in no wise pass from the law, till all be fulfilled. (Matthew 5:18) The law is not for the sake of humiliation, but rather for redeeming from sin and giving liberty. Jesus came to the Word, the law, in the flesh.

Knowing the truth,

the truth will set you free.

John 8:32

The Millennium Kingdom

There will be a restoration of the Word as well as physical restoration of nature at the time. As the water covers the sea, the knowledge of God will be full of the whole world. We will learn to know God from where the sun rises to where it goes down. All the secrets from Genesis to Revelation will be solved. At that time, the word will be seen more clearly as if the handkerchief that covered your eyes were removed. Jesus will be the King of Jerusalem and will rule the world with love and justice.

At that time, capitalism disappears, and a new economic system established by the Law is created so that everyone would live well without any shortage. Only then the sabbatical year and the jubilee will be appropriately kept. The Sabbatical year and Jubilee are God's perfect economic system that allows people and nature to coexist and live together.

The Millennium Kingdom provides all energy and food resources free of charge. People live in a house built by themselves, and they do not buy another's home. People can eat beautiful fruits every month, and they can keep their health with the leaves of trees that grow near the riverside. People have the privilege of traveling around the world on their horse. Every country can be visited freely without any visa restrictions, and at any place, they will be treated like a king. The Millennium kingdom will be harvested without any planting because the land and the sea will be recovered correctly. The food is overflowing, so people will be generous. The axis of the earth is restored, and it will have cool weather through all seasons. Thus, four seasons will be disappeared. Predators will become gentle, and human beings and nature will be one. The bird will not fear man and the snake will not bite children.

Those who are left behind will meet Jesus in Jerusalem

who governs the planet earth. People will enjoy the privilege of seeing the political Messiah in person. Jesus will be the greatest king in earth's history, and his people will experience happiness. Jesus will do politics with justice and love, and everyone will rejoice in his reign. During the millennium, the wicked disappear, but some bad men will be cursed and be pushed to live below a hundred years old. Those who are left will enjoy the privilege of learning and enjoying the completion of the Bible during the Millennium kingdom. People will study the process of fulfilling all Bible prophecy in detail. They will be fortunate to experience and realize the meaning of the Revelation of John. Those who are left will be living in an era where they can learn the Bible most accurately and adequately.

Those who are left will have a long life. The world is so broad, and people will know how many beautiful places exist. A thousand years may not be enough for living in every part of the globe even though people try spending only a single month for each site. Those left over the millennium will see to the end of earth science. People will enjoy cutting-edge scientific civilization. At this time, they will be provided with the best convenience and service that never imagined before. But since all culture is centered on God's Word, it will be full of acknowledging the glory of Jehovah as the waters cover the sea. Those who have left will experience the completion of the family system. People will have many children and descendants, and they will not find family destruction and divorce courts. By one husband and wife joining together, a holy family will be born in Jesus. Those who are left will receive the privilege of enjoying all these things in due time. It is the reward and crown of joy to those who have won.

However, when the time comes, the holy ones who have lived with Jesus and the body of the resurrection will disappear. As Satan is rereleased from the abyss, this land will be once again in chaos. With Satan's deceiving, humans deny God still, and people are divided into sheep and goats. The center of the world, Israel, and it's the farthest place called Gog and Magog are deceived by Satan, and a fight takes place. The city of Jerusalem, where the believers are gathered, surrounded by the enemy and are in danger. But God's fire comes down and burns all the enemies.

The Millennium Kingdom Features	Earth's recovery (extended life), Ezekiel temple, there are the sea and the sun, after Satan's released Gog and Magog war begins
The White Throne Judgment Features	The second resurrection of the dead, by book of life they are fallen into the lake of fire, or moved into new heaven and earth
The New Heaven and New Earth Features	Only heaven (New Jerusalem) has a tree of life, no temple, no sea, and no sun.

New Heaven and New Earth

When the Millennium Kingdom is over, the earth and the universe will be disappeared. Outside of the world, there is a massive throne of God. Isaiah saw the throne of the elevated God, saying that the temple was full of God's garments. Isaiah could not see the enormous image of God but saw only a part of his skirt. In front of God's sizeable white throne, there is a place like a vast glassy sea where the dead are resurrected and judged. At the white throne, the judges have recorded in the book of life which based on the data from the book of acts. The final judgment is up to God. In the end, some names would be erased in the book of life because of their sins and fall into the lake of fire. With that reason, some ministers and religious people would fall into the lake of fire. Those who were used for the gospel at first and deteriorated later to fall into the lake of fire are truly sad.

Those who are written in the book of life will be taken to New heaven and New earth. Only those who are rewarded can enter the city of heaven, which they call the New Jerusalem. The rest live in the new land and live with the human king. Those who have the reward will be able to taste the fruits of the trees that have been fed with the water of life flowing in the city of heaven. Only those who eat the fruit from the tree of life will be able to live forever. The city of Heaven is made of a cube, and its size is twelve thousand furlongs (about 2,400 km) in width, height, and height. There is no temple or sun in the city of heaven. Because the Lord is the temple and the sun, the city of heaven will be a flying world. People will live like angels wearing holy white robes. Holy white raiment is a complete material that transcends cleanliness, cold, heat, shock, gravity, and so on. There will be no tears, deaths, sorrow, crying, or sickness again. Heaven will be a beautiful place that we cannot even imagine.

This book is not written for the perfect human beings, but for the frail believers who struggle to be holy. I wanted to give them the hope and comfort of the rapture. I also want to challenge for Christians who are not adequately prepared as Lord's Brides. This book is for myself and my loved ones. We do not know when Jesus will return, but we hope him to come in the next Jubilee Year because the Jubilee is the year of joy in the Bible.

I wrote the book called "Timetable of God, TIMELINE" while writing this book "Left Behind." In Daniel's, the Gospels, and the Revelation, there is a mention that in the pre and post three and a half years; there was a common passage through when the plumb line is placed. The following are things that will happen at that time.

1. Divided into tribulation and great tribulation.

2. Separated from the raptors and those left behind.

3. The regime change of the Dragon and the Beast is done.

4. Two witnesses are martyred, and the four hundred and forty-four thousand of them died, and they were resurrected and raptured within three and a half days.

5. The abomination of destruction stood in the Third Temple, and the armies of the Beast destroyed the sacrifices and set up idols in the most Holy Place.

6. False prophets cause people to receive the mark of the beast in the human forehead and hands, forcing them to worship idols.

At this time the church expressed as a woman gives the birth to the holy believers, and they get raptured. But the woman, with her remaining children, fled to the wilderness and received training of fire for three and a half years. The woman is a wilderness church, and her offspring are the ones left behind. Those who have been left behind for forty-two months have been avoiding the Beast and have felt the threat of life. Also, natural calamities will cause many sufferings. But the target of the vial disasters is not the left ones, but the Beast and his army. Those who are left behind will receive greater protection and special grace from God.

I hope that readers of this book will become a holy people and participate in the Rapture. But do not be discouraged even if you are left behind, and remember the things in this book. I pray that you will find God in times of trouble and not lose hope.

Behold, I come quickly;
And my reward is with me,
to give every man according as his work shall be
- Revelation 22:12